Assessment

 Assessing the Common Core State Standards

Mc
Graw
Hill
Education

Bothell, WA • Chicago, IL • Columbus, OH • New York, NY

Cover: Nathan Love

www.mheonline.com/readingwonderworks

Copyright © McGraw-Hill Education

Send all inquiries to:
McGraw-Hill Education
Two Penn Plaza
New York, New York 10121

ISBN: 978-0-02-129749-8
MHID: 0-02-129749-5

Printed in the United States of America.

3 4 5 6 7 8 9 RHR 18 17 16 15 14

TABLE OF CONTENTS

Weekly Assessment

Mid-Unit Assessment

Unit Assessment

Exit Assessment

TABLE OF CONTENTS

Oral Reading Fluency Assessment

Scoring Sheets

Answer Keys

Assessment

The *Assessment* BLM is an integral part of the complete assessment program aligned with the Common Core State Standards (CCSS) and the core reading and intervention curriculums of *McGraw-Hill Reading WonderWorks* and *McGraw-Hill Reading Wonders.*

Purpose of *Assessment*

The instruction in *McGraw-Hill Reading WonderWorks* is parallel to the instruction in *McGraw-Hill Reading Wonders*. Student results in *Assessment* provide a picture of achievement within *McGraw-Hill Reading WonderWorks* and a signal as to whether students can successfully transition back to Approaching Level reading instruction.

Assessment offers the opportunity to monitor student progress in a steady and structured manner while providing formative assessment data.

As students complete each week of the intervention program, they will be assessed on their understanding of weekly vocabulary words and their ability to access and comprehend complex literary and informational selections using text evidence.

At the key 3-week and 6-week reporting junctures, assessments measure student understanding of previously-taught vocabulary words and comprehension skills and provide evidence of student progress through the curriculum. If students show a level of mastery at the end of a unit, an assessment to exit out of *McGraw-Hill Reading WonderWorks* and into the Approaching Level instruction of *McGraw-Hill Reading Wonders* is available.

Throughout the unit, oral reading fluency passages are available to measure student ability to read connected text fluently, accurately, and with a measure of prosody.

The results of the assessments provided in *Assessment* can be used to inform subsequent instruction and assist with grouping and leveling designations.

Components of *Assessment*

- Weekly Assessment
- Mid-Unit Assessment
- Unit Assessment
- Exit Assessment
- Oral Reading Fluency Assessment

Assessment focuses on key areas of English Language Arts as identified by the CCSS—Reading, Language, and Fluency. To assess Reading and Language proficiency, students read selections and respond to items focusing on comprehension skills, vocabulary words, literary elements, and text features. These items assess the ability to access meaning from the text and demonstrate understanding of words and phrases. To assess Fluency, students read passages for one minute to measure their words correct per minute (WCPM) and accuracy rates.

Weekly Assessment

The Weekly Assessment features a "cold read" reading selection (informational or narrative based on the weekly reading focus) and 5 items—three items on the weekly comprehension skill and two items that ask students to show how context helps them identify the meaning of a vocabulary word. (For weeks in which poetry is the featured genre, vocabulary items are replaced by items assessing literary elements.) Students will provide text evidence to support their answers.

Administering Weekly Assessment

Each test should be administered once the instruction for the specific week is completed. Make a copy of the assessment and the Scoring Sheet for each student. The Scoring Sheet allows for informal comments on student responses and adds to an understanding of strengths and weaknesses.

After each student has a copy of the assessment, provide a version of the following directions: Say: *Write your name and the date on the question pages for this assessment.* (When students are finished, continue with the directions.) *You will read a selection and answer questions about it. Read the selection and the questions that follow it carefully. Write your responses on the lines provided. Go back to the text to underline and circle the text evidence that supports your answers. When you have completed the assessment, put your pencil down and turn the pages over. You may begin now.*

Answer procedural questions during the assessment, but do not provide any assistance on the items or selections. After the class has completed the assessment, ask students to verify that their names and the date are written on the necessary pages.

Alternatively, you may choose to work through the assessment with the students. This will provide an additional opportunity for you to observe their ability to access complex text in a more informal group setting.

Evaluating the Weekly Assessment

Each Weekly Assessment is worth 10 points, with each item worth 2 points. Use the scoring rubric below to assign a point total per item. A Weekly Answer Key is provided to help with scoring. Student results should provide a clear picture of their understanding of the weekly comprehension skill and the weekly vocabulary words. Reteach tested skills if assessment results point to a clear deficiency.

Weekly Assessment Scoring Rubric	
Score	**Description**
2	• Reasonable, clear, and specific • Supported by accurate and relevant text evidence • Shows ability to access complex text
1	• Reasonable but somewhat unclear or vague • Supported by general, incomplete, partially accurate, or partially relevant text evidence • Shows some ability to access complex text
0	• Incorrect, unreasonable, or too vague to understand • Not supported by relevant text evidence • Shows no understanding of how to access complex text

Evidence may be specific words from the text or a paraphrase.

Mid-Unit Assessment

The Mid-Unit Assessment presents a snapshot of student understanding at the key 3-week instructional interval. This test features two "cold read" reading selections and 10 selected response items—seven items on the featured comprehension skills in Weeks 1–3 and three items that ask students to show how context helps them identify the meaning of a vocabulary word.

Administering Mid-Unit Assessment

Each test should be administered at the end of Week 3 instruction. Make a copy of the assessment and the Scoring Sheet for each student.

After each student has a copy of the assessment, provide a version of the following directions: Say: *Write your name and the date on the question pages for this assessment.* (When students are finished, continue with the directions.) *You will read two selections and answer questions about them. Read the selections and the questions that follow them carefully. Choose the correct answer to each question and completely fill in the bubble next to it. When you have completed the assessment, put your pencil down and turn the pages over. You may begin now.*

NOTE: The directions above can be used when students take the Unit and Exit Assessments.

Evaluating the Mid-Unit Assessment

Each Mid-Unit Assessment is worth 10 points, with each item worth 1 point. An Answer Key is provided to help with scoring. Note student success or difficulty with specific skills. Use this data to determine the instructional focus going forward. Reteach tested skills for students who score 5 points or less on the comprehension items and 2 points or less on the vocabulary items.

Unit and Exit Assessment

The Unit Assessment tests student mastery of the key instructional content featured in the unit. This test features two "cold read" reading selections (one narrative text and one informational text) and 15 selected response items—ten items on the unit's comprehension skills and five items that ask students to show how context helps them identify the meaning of a vocabulary word.

The Exit Assessment is a "parallel" test to the Unit Assessment. It assesses the same skills and pool of vocabulary words using the same format. The key differentiator between the tests is the higher level of text complexity featured in the reading selections, a level more in line with the rigor found in Approaching Level *McGraw-Hill Reading Wonders* materials.

Moving from Unit to Exit Assessment

Administer the Unit Assessment to ALL students at the close of unit instruction. Make a copy of the assessment and the Scoring Sheet for each student. Each Unit Assessment is worth 15 points, with each item worth 1 point. An Answer Key is provided to help with scoring.

If students score 13 or higher on the Unit Assessment, administer the Exit Assessment. The Exit Assessment is ONLY for those students who reach this Unit Assessment benchmark.

Oral Reading Fluency Assessment

Fluency passages are included to help assess the level at which students have progressed beyond decoding into comprehension. When readers can read the words in connected text automatically, they are free to focus on using the critical thinking skills essential to constructing meaning from complex text.

24 fiction and nonfiction passages are included to help you assess fluency. The passages are set in three Unit/Lexile bands—the first set of eight is for Units 1 and 2, the next set of eight is for Units 3 and 4, and the final set of eight is for Units 5 and 6.

See pages 6 and 7 of *Fluency Assessment* for directions on administering and scoring oral reading fluency passages and for the unit-specific benchmark WCPM scores.

Transitioning into *McGraw-Hill Reading Wonders* Instruction

Moving students into Approaching Level *McGraw-Hill Reading Wonders* instruction at the completion of a unit should be guided by assessment data, student performance during the unit instruction, and informal observation of student progress.

Use the following assessment criteria to help judge student readiness for Approaching Level designation and materials:

• Unit Assessment score of 13 or higher

• Ability to comprehend and analyze the Level Up Approaching Leveled Reader

• Score of 3 or higher on Level Up Write About Reading assignment

• Mastery of the unit benchmark skills in the Foundational Skills Kit and *Reading Wonders* Adaptive Learning

• WCPM score and accuracy rate that meet or exceed the unit goals

• Exit Assessment score of 13 or higher

Weekly
Assessment

Name: _____ Date: _____

**Read "The Princess and the Giant Bridge" before you answer
Numbers 1 through 5.**

The Princess and the Giant Bridge

Long ago, a princess lived in a castle by a river.
One day, a huge storm came. When the storm passed,
the princess had disappeared.

The king and queen searched wildly and **frantically**.
"I fear the princess is gone!" cried the queen.

The river had carried the princess away. She was far
from the castle. So the princess set out to find her way
home. She walked for two days. Then she saw the castle
across the river.

"I must think about a way to get to the other side,"
she said. The princess sat down to **brainstorm**. Soon, she
heard loud footsteps. Looking up, she saw a giant.

"I can help," said the giant. First, he went into the
river and floated on his back. Then, he stretched his
fingertips to one side and his toes to the other. At last,
the princess was able to run across the bridge that the
giant had made.

When the princess got home, the king and queen
were filled with joy. They all lived happily ever after.

GO ON →

**Use "The Princess and the Giant Bridge" to answer
Numbers 1 through 5.**

1 **Circle** the word that helps you understand what
frantically means.

2 What is the first thing the princess does after the river
carries her away?

_____

3 What does *brainstorm* mean?

_____

Circle the sentence that tells why the princess
must *brainstorm*.

4 **Underline** the sentence that tells what happens right
before the princess sees the giant.

5 **Draw a box** around what the giant does after he floats
on his back in the river.

What word tells you that the giant does this next?

_____

STOP

**Read "Soccer Buddies" before you answer Numbers 1
through 5.**

Soccer Buddies

Becky and Kim were best friends who did everything
together. "I just signed up for the soccer team," said Becky.
"Did you sign up yet?"

Kim **hesitated** for a few seconds. Then she said, "No,
I don't think I'm going to join this year. I'd like to play on
the team, but I'm not good enough."

"You are good enough!" said Becky. "You have to
believe in yourself. You need to get some **self-esteem**. Meet
me at my house after school. Bring your soccer ball."

When Kim got to Becky's house, they went out to the
backyard. Becky set up a soccer net and some cones. First,
she helped Kim practice moving the ball with her feet.
Then, they practiced kicking.

The two friends practiced every afternoon for the next
few days. Finally, Kim decided to join the team after all.
Her teammates were glad she did. At their first game, Kim
scored the winning goal. When everyone cheered, Kim
hugged Becky. "Thanks," she said. "I feel pretty good about
my soccer skills now!"

GO ON →

Name: _____ Date: _____

Use "Soccer Buddies" to answer Numbers 1 through 5.

1 **Underline** the sentence in the second paragraph that states Kim's problem.

2 **Circle** the clues that tell what *hesitated* means.

What is the meaning of *hesitated*?

_____

3 How does Becky try to help Kim solve her problem?

_____

_____

Draw a box around the detail that shows what Becky does first.

4 **Circle** the words that help you understand what *self-esteem* means.

5 How do you know that Kim solves her problem?

_____

_____

Underline the sentence that shows how Kim feels when her problem is solved.

STOP

Copyright © McGraw-Hill Education. Permission is granted to reproduce for classroom use.

Name: _____ Date: _____

Read "Natural Disasters" before you answer Numbers 1 through 5.

Natural Disasters

Hurricanes and earthquakes are natural disasters. They can quickly change the surface of Earth. Some changes are similar for both hurricanes and earthquakes. Other changes are not.

Hurricanes are powerful storms that start over warm ocean waters. Hurricanes can cause great **destruction**. They bring strong winds and floods. The winds can tear up trees and buildings. The floods can destroy beaches and roads.

Unlike hurricanes, earthquakes start inside Earth. They shake the ground. This shaking can cause buildings and roads to crumble and **collapse**.

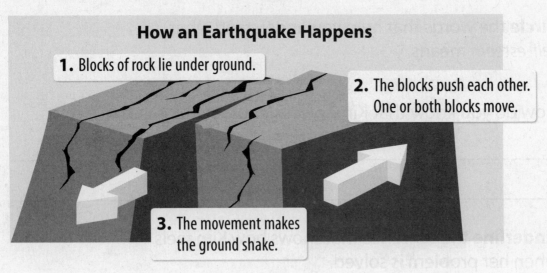

How an Earthquake Happens

1. Blocks of rock lie under ground.

2. The blocks push each other. One or both blocks move.

3. The movement makes the ground shake.

Can we stop natural disasters? No, we cannot. But we can plan what to do when they happen. An emergency plan can help people stay safe.

GO ON →

Name: _____ Date: _____

Use "Natural Disasters" to answer Numbers 1 through 5.

1 **Draw a box** around the sentences that tell how hurricanes and earthquakes are alike.

2 **Underline** examples of *destruction* caused by hurricanes.

Write the meaning of *destruction*.

_____

3 How are hurricanes and earthquakes different?

_____

_____

Draw a box around the clue word that shows they are different.

4 **Underline** the word that means about the same as *collapse*.

What is the meaning of *collapse*?

_____

5 Look at the diagram. **Circle** the information in the diagram that is also in the passage.

STOP

Read "Rita the Rock Star" before you answer Numbers 1 through 5.

Rita the Rock Star

Rita was happy because she was going to learn to play a musical instrument. But first she had to pick one. Her mother said, "Let's go to the music store. You can learn about some instruments there."

The Science of Music

There were many instruments at the store. Rita liked the French horn because of its shape. "How does it work?" she asked.

"Sound is made when an object vibrates," said the storeowner. He pointed to the mouthpiece. "You put your lips here and buzz," he said. "That makes air vibrate down long tubes. And that's what makes the sound."

For one **thrilling** moment, Rita held the French horn. It was exciting! She liked the way it looked and felt.

A Decision to Make

Rita thought about the French horn on the way home. Maybe she would pick that instrument. She had time to decide. She dreamed of becoming a musician with great **capabilities**. Rita wanted to learn skills so that she could be in a rock band someday!

GO ON →

Name: _____ Date: _____

Use "Rita the Rock Star" to answer Numbers 1 through 5.

1 Why do Rita and her mother go to the music store?

_____

Underline the sentence that tells the cause.

2 Find the section "The Science of Music." **Draw a box** around what happens when an object vibrates.

3 **Circle** a word that means about the same as *thrilling*.

4 What causes air to vibrate in a French horn?

_____

_____

Underline the cause.

5 **Circle** a clue word that tells you what *capabilities* are.

Write the meaning of *capabilities*.

_____

STOP

Read "Kids Helping Kids" before you answer Numbers 1 through 5.

Kids Helping Kids

Kids Helping Kids (KHK) is a new kind of organization, or group. Its name describes why it is so **innovative**. This organization is run by kids. It is a not-for-profit group, which means it does not want to make money. It teaches kids how to help others. Kids also learn many things about themselves.

How Does it Work?

KHK teaches kids to be leaders. Kids of all backgrounds learn skills. They take part in projects that help others. Young people are in charge of the projects. This teaches kids many things. They learn what they like to do and how to lead others. They also learn the importance of helping others.

What's Next for KHK?

Kids Helping Kids is planning a new **enterprise**. It wants to help kids around the world get clean water. The group is working hard to figure out a way to do this.

When kids in this group grow up, they will have the skills to do great things. They will become leaders of tomorrow!

GO ON →

Use "Kids Helping Kids" to answer Numbers 1 through 5.

1 **Underline** clue words that help you understand the meaning of *innovative*.

What makes Kids Helping Kids an *innovative* group?

_____

_____

2 What is the main idea of the first paragraph?

_____

_____

3 **Draw a box** around the heading for the section that tells what KHK does.

Who takes part in KHK?

_____

4 **Circle** three things that kids learn from KHK projects.

5 **Underline** the sentence that explains the new *enterprise* KHK is planning.

What does *enterprise* mean?

_____

STOP

Read "The Spider and the Honey Tree" before you answer Numbers 1 through 5.

The Spider and the Honey Tree

Long ago, there was a girl who knew where to pick the best fruit in her village. A spider promised to keep the girl's secret if she took him to the fruit. The girl believed the spider was being **honest** and truthful, so she agreed.

First, the girl took the spider to a plum tree. He jumped on the plums and ate all of them.

Then, the girl took the spider to a banana tree. He jumped on the bananas and ate them, too.

The girl could not believe the spider's **greed**! He did not share anything!

Next, the girl took the spider to a tree and pointed to a small hole. "Inside is delicious honey," she said.

The spider jumped in and ate all the honey. When he tried to come out, he was stuck. He had eaten so much that he could not fit through the hole.

"Help!" the spider cried.

"Absolutely not!" said the girl. "You are stuck because you ate too much! You should have left some for others."

The spider promised to take only what he needed from then on.

GO ON →

Weekly Assessment · Unit 2, Week 1

Name: _____ **Date:** _____

Use "The Spider and the Honey Tree" to answer Numbers 1 through 5.

1 **Underline** the word in the text that tells what *honest* means.

2 What does the spider want the girl to do at the beginning of the passage?

_____

3 **Underline** examples in the text of the spider's *greed*.

What does *greed* mean?

_____

4 **Circle** where the girl takes the spider at the end of the passage.

Tell why she does this.

_____

_____

5 **Draw a box** around what happens to the spider at the end of the passage.

What lesson does the spider learn?

_____

_____

STOP

Read "Squirrel and Raccoon" before you answer Numbers 1 through 5.

Squirrel and Raccoon

CHARACTERS: Squirrel; Raccoon

Scene I

(It is late at night in a backyard. Squirrel is sleeping. Raccoon knocks over a trashcan while searching for food. This wakes up Squirrel and puts him in a bad mood.)

SQUIRREL: *(Angrily)* You woke me again! Why do you make so much noise at night?

RACCOON: Please don't be so **cranky**. I am just trying to find some food. This is the time that I eat.

SQUIRREL: *(Yawning)* Well, please try not to bang the lids and make such a **commotion**. Why don't I gather food for you during the day? You can eat it at night instead of looking through trashcans. Then we will both be happy.

Scene II

(It is early evening the next day in the same backyard. Raccoon is waking up. Squirrel is getting ready to go to sleep.)

RACCOON: *(Happily)* Look at all this food you left for me! Thanks, my friend. Now I can eat and you can sleep in peace.

SQUIRREL: *(Smiling)* You're welcome. If we work as a team, then we can solve both of our problems!

GO ON →

Use "Squirrel and Raccoon" to answer Numbers 1 through 5.

1 **Circle** the clues that help you know what *cranky* means.

Write the meaning of *cranky*.

_____

2 What is the problem at the beginning of Scene I?

_____

_____

3 **Circle** the details that tell what Raccoon does to make a *commotion*.

What does *commotion* mean?

_____

_____

4 What does Squirrel do to help Raccoon?

_____

_____

Underline the details that tell why he does this.

5 What lesson do Squirrel and Raccoon learn in Scene II?

_____

_____

STOP

Name: _____   Date: _____

Read "Butterfly Garden" before you answer Numbers 1 through 5.

Butterfly Garden

Natural History Museum

Luis and his mom enjoy going to the natural history museum. They learn about dinosaurs and other **extinct** animals there. Today, they will see some animals that still exist. They are going to the museum's butterfly garden.

They walk along a path. There are colorful plants and butterflies. "This sign says butterflies live all around the world," says Mom. "They have always **flourished**, or done well, in warmer climates."

"That's why it is so warm in here!" says Luis.

Butterflies in Action

Luis reads another sign. It says that butterflies are active during the day. They fly from plant to plant. They sip nectar from flowers.

Then a butterfly lands on Luis's shoulder. "My yellow shirt! The butterfly must think it is a flower!"

Butterflies are part of a food chain.

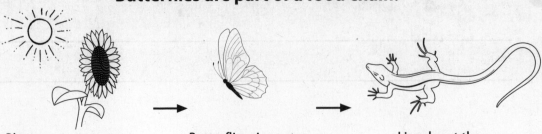

Plants use energy to grow flowers.   Butterflies sip nectar from flowers.   Lizards eat the butterflies.

GO ON →

Name: _____ Date: _____

Use "Butterfly Garden" to answer Numbers 1 through 5.

1 **Circle** an example of something that is *extinct*.

Which words in the text mean the opposite of *extinct*?

_____

2 Look at the section "Natural History Museum." Tell where butterflies live.

_____

3 **Circle** the words that tell the meaning of *flourished*.

4 Look at the section "Butterflies in Action." **Underline** two details that tell what butterflies do during the day.

What is the MAIN idea of this section?

_____

_____

5 What does the flow chart show about butterflies?

_____

_____

Draw a box around the sentence that tells the MAIN idea of the flow chart.

STOP

Read "Animal Camouflage" before you answer Numbers 1 through 5.

Animal Camouflage

Animal Survival

How do some animals stay safe in the wild? They can be **camouflaged**. The color or shape of the animals helps them look like part of their surroundings. This makes them hard to see. They stay safe from **predators** who hunt the animals for food.

Many Kinds of Camouflage

Animals use different kinds of camouflage. Body color helps some animals blend in with their surroundings. Polar bears, for example, are covered in white fur. This makes them hard to see in the snow.

Other animals have special patterns or markings. Spots or stripes make them hard to see in different environments. Zebras, tigers, and some fish use this kind of camouflage.

Some animals blend in because they look like other things. Some insects look like sticks, leaves, or thorns. It is easy for them to hide in the plants they live on.

There are different kinds of camouflage. But one thing is the same. Camouflage helps animals survive!

GO ON →

Name: _____ Date: _____

Use "Animal Camouflage" to answer Numbers 1 through 5.

1 **Draw a box** around animals with special markings that make them hard to see.

2 **Circle** the sentences in the article that help you understand the meaning of *camouflaged*.

What does *camouflaged* mean?

_____

3 **Underline** key details that tell how animals can be camouflaged.

4 **Circle** the clues that tell what a *predator* does.

What does *predator* mean?

_____

5 What is the MAIN idea of the section "Many Kinds of Camouflage"?

_____

_____

STOP

**Read "The Tiger and the Monkey" before you answer
Numbers 1 through 5.**

The Tiger and the Monkey

A playful monkey, brown and little

Was trapped upon a vine, so brittle,

The tiger said, "You will be mine!

As soon as I can break this vine!"

And so the tiger scratched and prowled,

And all the while his stomach growled.

The monkey acted like a clown,

He danced and laughed as he looked down.

At last, the tiger with outstretched claws

Lay down a moment to take a pause.

While resting, he looked up and found

The monkey holding something round.

The little monkey threw below

A coconut at Tiger's toe!

Poor Tiger cried, "That's it, I'm through!

I'll eat this coconut, not you!"

GO ON →

Name: _____ Date: _____

Use "The Tiger and the Monkey" to answer Numbers 1 through 5.

1 How do you know "The Tiger and the Monkey" is a lyric poem?

_____

_____

2 **Underline** two words that rhyme in the first stanza of the poem.

3 **Circle** the simile in the second stanza.

What two unlike things are being compared?

_____

4 Is the speaker a character in the poem? Explain how you know.

_____

_____

5 What does the speaker think about the tiger at the end of the poem?

_____

Draw a box around a clue that tells you how the speaker feels about the tiger.

STOP

Read "Fast Friends" before you answer Numbers 1 through 5.

Fast Friends

Padma was bored toward the end of winter break. One day, she found a box with a **jumble** of different items inside. "What is this?" she asked her mom.

"It is a mess of things I bought at a yard sale," Mom said. "You may look through it, but do it **cautiously** in case there is something sharp inside."

Inside the box, Padma found a worn frame with a picture of a girl her age. She wiped off the frame and when she looked up, the girl from the picture was standing next to her!

"I'm Olivia," said the girl. "Do you want to play?"

Padma thought it was strange to play with someone from a picture frame! Still, she did not want to hurt the girl's feelings. She and Olivia quickly became good friends.

Soon, winter break ended. Back at school, Padma missed her new friend. Suddenly, her teacher said, "We have a new student today, so let's all welcome her."

Padma looked up. It was Olivia! Padma grinned and thought, "This is amazing!"

GO ON →

Use "Fast Friends" to answer Numbers 1 through 5.

1 **Underline** the words in the text that tell the meaning of *jumble*.

What does *jumble* mean?

_____

2 Is the passage told in the first-person or third-person point of view?

_____

Circle the pronouns in the first paragraph that support your answer.

3 **Underline** the clues in the text that help you understand the meaning of *cautiously*.

What does it mean to do something *cautiously*?

_____

4 What does Padma think when the girl in the picture comes to life?

_____

_____

5 **Underline** how Padma feels when she learns that Olivia will be in her class.

Read "New Shoes" before you answer Numbers 1 through 5.

New Shoes

Joe and I both wanted to take part in a community service project. One day, I noticed Joe was wearing new sneakers. "I have an idea," I said. "Let's collect old sneakers."

Joe looked confused. He asked, "What are you thinking, Max? What can we possibly do with smelly old sneakers?"

"We can recycle them," I said. "I read about a program that collects old sneakers. They grind the sneakers into small pieces that are used to make playground surfaces."

"That's great," said Joe. "Where do we start, and when?"

Joe is a good artist, so right away I **assigned** him the task of making posters. "The people who live in our town must have old sneakers," I said. "The posters will tell **residents** where to drop off their shoes." We talked about putting collection boxes in school, too.

It felt good to be helping the community. We knew our project would be a success, and we'd be helping planet Earth, too!

GO ON →

Use "New Shoes" to answer Numbers 1 through 5.

1 Is the passage told in the first-person or third-person point of view?

_____

Underline the pronoun in the first paragraph that shows who is telling the story.

2 **Circle** the details in the text that tell what Max *assigned* Joe.

What does *assigned* mean?

_____

3 How does Max feel about community service?

_____

_____

4 **Circle** the clues in the text that help you understand the meaning of *residents*.

5 How does Max feel about the project at the end of the passage?

_____

_____

Draw a box around the details that show how he feels.

STOP

Read "Sandra Day O'Connor" before you answer Numbers 1 through 5.

Sandra Day O'Connor

Sandra Day O'Connor was born in Texas in 1930. She graduated from law school in 1952. She had a hard time getting a job as a lawyer even though she was well **qualified**. She was able to do the job as well as any man. But at that time women did not have the same opportunities as men. As a result, it took her longer to start working as a lawyer.

Making History

In 1981, Sandra Day O'Connor did something wonderful. She became a judge in the United States Supreme Court. She was the first female Supreme Court judge. This gave **encouragement** to women everywhere. It gave them hope that they could be as successful as men.

Sandra Day O'Connor was a judge on important cases. She tried to protect the rights of Americans. She helped to create laws that were fair for everyone.

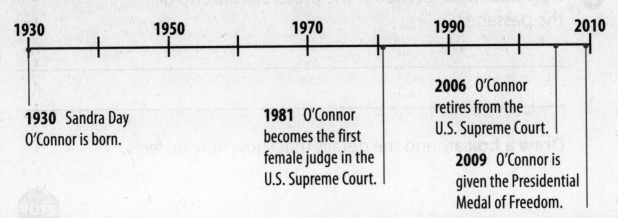

1930   1950   1970   1990   2010

1930 Sandra Day O'Connor is born.

1981 O'Connor becomes the first female judge in the U.S. Supreme Court.

2006 O'Connor retires from the U.S. Supreme Court.

2009 O'Connor is given the Presidential Medal of Freedom.

GO ON →

Weekly Assessment · Unit 3, Week 3

Name: _____ Date: _____

Use "Sandra Day O'Connor" to answer Numbers 1 through 5.

1 **Draw a box** around the details that tell the meaning of *qualified*.

Why was O'Connor *qualified* to be a lawyer?

_____

_____

2 **Circle** the details that show how the author feels about O'Connor becoming a judge for the U.S. Supreme Court.

3 **Draw a box** around a word that means almost the SAME as *encouragement*.

How did O'Connor give *encouragement* to women?

_____

_____

4 How do you think the author feels about equal rights?

_____

_____

Underline the details in the article that support your answer.

5 Look at the time line. **Circle** the details that help to show O'Connor was an important woman in history.

STOP

Read "President John F. Kennedy" before you answer Numbers 1 through 5.

President John F. Kennedy

At age 43, John F. Kennedy did something amazing. He became the youngest person to be elected U. S. President.

Words to Inspire

President Kennedy took office on January 20, 1961. His **address** to the crowd showed that he felt strongly about public service. In his speech, he told Americans to do good things. People still remember his words today. He said, "Ask not what your country can do for you—ask what you can do for your country."

These words inspired many young people. It made them want to make a difference in the world. Many people wanted to go out and help others.

A Leader to Remember

President Kennedy was shot and killed in 1963. His death caused great sadness across the country. People's hopes were suddenly **shattered**. But they would not stay broken. Kennedy's time as president was short, but he worked hard to improve people's lives. His words led many others to do the same.

GO ON →

Use "President John F. Kennedy" to answer Numbers 1 through 5.

1 How does the author feel about John F. Kennedy becoming the youngest person elected U. S. President?

_____

2 **Circle** the clues in the text that tell the meaning of *address*.

What does *address* mean in this article?

_____

3 **Draw a box** around the words from President Kennedy's speech.

Why does the author think these words are important?

_____

_____

4 **Circle** the word that tells what *shattered* means.

5 What is the author's opinion about Kennedy as a leader?

_____

_____

Underline the text evidence in the last paragraph that supports your answer.

STOP

Read "Internet Safety" before you answer Numbers 1 through 5.

Internet Safety

Can you imagine life without the Internet? The idea for the Internet began in the 1960s. **Advancements** in science and technology made the Internet available to the public in the 1990s. Even more improvements have made it available almost everywhere today.

A Big Help

There are many good things about the Internet. People can use it to get information. Students can research school reports and find answers to questions they have about the world. People can even go to the Internet to get the daily news or to play games.

Some Problems

The Internet also has some dangers. Children may see material that is not good for them to read. They may tell too much about themselves by accident. They may use the Internet in ways they should not. These **concerns** cause parents to worry about their children's safety.

The Internet has changed the way we act in our world. To fully enjoy it, we must first learn about Internet safety.

GO ON →

Use "Internet Safety" to answer Numbers 1 through 5.

1 **Draw a box** around the question in the article.

Tell how the author feels about the use of the Internet.

_____

_____

2 **Underline** the text that tells what *advancements* have done for the Internet.

What does *advancements* mean?

_____

_____

3 **Circle** the author's opinion in the section "A Big Help."

4 **Underline** the clues that help you understand the meaning of *concerns*.

What does *concerns* mean?

_____

_____

5 At the end of the article, what does the author think is important for all of us to do?

_____

_____

STOP

Read "Education for All" before you answer Numbers 1 through 5.

Education for All

Imagine a world where most children do not go to school. Instead, they work in factories or on farms. Does this seem strange to you?

Long ago, there was no education system in the United States. Many children did not go to school. That is because there were no schools available. As a result, most children never learned how to read or write. They only learned if their parents taught them.

Soon, state governments started making decisions about education. In 1852, Massachusetts became the first state to pass public school **legislation** (lej•is•LAY•shuhn), or laws. Children between the ages of eight and fourteen had to attend school. Families paid a fine if their children did not go. By 1918, all states had laws like this. The laws were a **commitment**, or promise, to make sure that all children received an education.

Today, our country has a free public education system. It begins in kindergarten and goes up to 12th grade. Students learn many skills. After graduating, they can get jobs. Some decide to go to college. At college, they continue to learn.

GO ON →

Name: _____ Date: _____

Use "Education for All" to answer Numbers 1 through 5.

1 **Underline** why children did not go to school long ago.

What happened when they did not go to school?

_____

_____

2 **Circle** the text that shows how to pronounce *legislation*.

What does *legislation* mean?

_____

3 What happened if families did not obey the public school law in 1852?

_____

_____

4 **Circle** the word that restates what a *commitment* is.

5 Why can all children in the United States go to school today?

_____

_____

Draw a box around the word that shows all children can go.

STOP

Read "George Washington—in Person!" before you answer Numbers 1 through 5.

George Washington—in Person!

"What are you doing in the attic, Eva?" Mom shouted.

"Just looking for my bicycle pump," I shouted back.

I looked around and didn't find it, but I did see a dusty wooden chair, so I sat on the seat and spun around. Suddenly, I was surrounded by a bright light, and as I looked down, I saw that I was wearing a long hoop dress!

"Unbelievable—I was just wearing jeans!" I thought to myself. I spotted an old newspaper on the ground and picked it up.

It was dated 1789 and the headline read, "George Washington Becomes President." I read the article and learned that no one ran against Washington. He did not have an **opponent**. It sounded as if he did not have a **campaign**, either. He did not have to give speeches or do activities to get elected like today's presidents do.

Suddenly, I heard people cheering. I looked up and saw George Washington—in person! He was standing on a balcony giving a speech about protecting our nation.

"Wow!" I said to myself. I couldn't wait to get home and tell my mother what I just saw.

Use "George Washington—in Person!" to answer Numbers 1 through 5.

1 **Draw a box** around the clues that tell who the narrator is.

What is the name of the narrator?

_____

2 **Underline** the details that show how the narrator feels after finding herself in a hoop dress.

Why does the narrator feel this way?

_____

_____

3 **Circle** the words that tell the meaning of *opponent*.

4 **Circle** the clues that describe a president's *campaign*.

What does *campaign* mean?

_____

5 **Underline** the details that tell how the narrator feels about seeing George Washington.

STOP

Read "Dreaming of the Model T" before you answer Numbers 1 through 5.

Dreaming of the Model T

"Matthew, eat your breakfast," his mother said again.

Matthew looked up from the newspaper and said, "Henry Ford's Model T car is fantastic! Right now it costs $850, but it will cost much less in five years. It is being built on an assembly line—I can't wait to buy one someday!"

On the way to school, Matthew **scouted** for a Model T by looking down Main Street and then searching the side streets. When he walked around the corner, he spotted one with dirt smudges on it from the muddy streets. "I wonder who owns it," thought Matthew. "I could make it spotless!"

After school, he saw Lizzie Bond get into the same Model T beside her father, so he rushed up to them.

"Hi, Lizzie. Hi, Mr. Bond!"

"How are you?" Mr. Bond smiled.

"Good! I…ummm…was wondering…"

"What is it, son?" asked Mr. Bond.

"Could I wash your Model T every Saturday? I'd make it so it was **gleaming**, just like a diamond!"

"That's a great idea, and I'll even pay you for it."

As the Model T pulled away, Matthew was one step closer to getting his very own car.

GO ON →

Use "Dreaming of the Model T" to answer Numbers 1 through 5.

1 Is the narrator a character in the passage? Explain how you know.

_____

_____

2 **Draw a box** around the clues that show how Matthew feels about the Model T car.

3 **Circle** the details that explain what *scouted* means.

What does *scouted* mean?

_____

4 How do you know that Matthew is nervous about asking Mr. Bond something?

_____

_____

Underline the sentence that supports your answer.

5 **Circle** the details that tell the meaning of *gleaming*.

What does *gleaming* mean?

_____

STOP

Read "Astronomy Club" before you answer Numbers 1 through 5.

Astronomy Club

Do you like to stargaze? If so, you might be a future **astronomer**. This is a scientist who studies the night sky. You can learn about the sky now, while you are still a kid. There are many astronomy clubs for kids on the Internet. You might even find a club in your community.

An astronomer uses a tool called a **telescope**. This tube-shaped instrument helps you view distant objects. A simple telescope has a few main parts. You look through an eyepiece. Inside the telescope, there is a lens that makes objects in the sky look bigger than they actually are. There is also a focuser, or knob that you turn, that helps objects look clear, not fuzzy. Finally, the telescope is placed on a tripod. This is a stand that keeps the telescope steady so it does not move around.

Did you know that our planet moves in a circle around the Sun? As a result, day turns to night. Nighttime is the perfect time for an astronomy club to meet. So, get out your telescope. Enjoy what you see in the night sky!

Parts of a Telescope

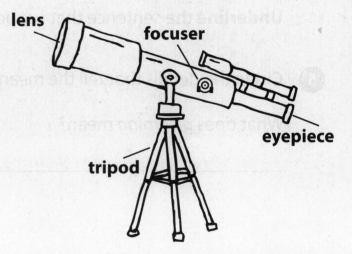

Use "Astronomy Club" to answer Numbers 1 through 5.

1 **Circle** the sentence that tells what an *astronomer* is.

2 What is the result of turning a focuser knob on
a telescope?

_____

_____

3 **Circle** the details that tell what a *telescope* helps you do.

What is a *telescope*?

_____

4 What is the purpose of the diagram?

_____

_____

Draw a box around the telescope part that you look
into to see objects in the night sky.

5 **Underline** what causes day to turn to night.

Why is this good for astronomers?

_____

_____

STOP

Read "STOP!" before you answer Numbers 1 through 5.

STOP!

Walking home from school each day

    my friends and I wave goodbye at Pine Road.

It is time to cross that big, wide street—

    An unsafe speedway where cars zoom past.

"STOP!" I think to myself. But no one hears me.

The cars zip by—I am a ghost to them.

Every day I think, "We need a STOP sign here."

I stand, hovering above the curb—staying put—

    wishing I could fly instead of walking across.

Finally, I get to the other side and arrive home safely.

I complain to Dad—and he agrees with me!

"We'll go to the town meeeting on Tuesday," he says.

"We'll make a video at Pine Road to show."

We must get the town council's attention.

Tuesday comes and we are ready.

We show the video. We present our plan.

"Put up STOP signs at Pine Road!"

The council members agree—the signs will go up!

I turn to my dad and make a "V" with two fingers—

    the sign of victory—and triumph. We did it!

Smiling, I think how cars will now "STOP!"

GO ON →

Name: _____ **Date:** _____

Use "STOP!" to answer Numbers 1 through 5.

1 **Draw a box** around the details in the *first* stanza that tell how the narrator feels about Pine Road.

2 Why does the narrator wish he could fly?

_____

_____

3 **Circle** the word that is repeated in the poem.

Why do you think this word is repeated?

_____

_____

4 **Underline** the details that show how the narrator is successful at the end of the poem.

What has changed since the *beginning* of the poem?

_____

_____

5 What story does the narrator tell in the poem?

_____

_____

_____

STOP

Read "Lucky" before you answer Numbers 1 through 5.

Lucky

Raj loved visiting his neighbor, Mrs. Brown. She lived alone with her dog, Lucky. Her house was filled with **portraits** of her children and grandchildren who lived far away. Raj liked looking at the photographs and listening to Mrs. Brown tell stories about her family.

One day, Mrs. Brown seemed sad. "I have to have hip surgery," she said. "I will be in the hospital for a few days. I have no one to care for Lucky, so he will have to stay in a kennel. He will miss being with people he knows."

"I will ask my parents if Lucky can stay at our house," Raj said.

Raj cared for Lucky while Mrs. Brown was gone. Then he brought Lucky back to her. When Lucky saw Mrs. Brown, he wagged his tail to **express** how happy he was.

Mrs. Brown needed to use a walker for a while to get around. She could not walk Lucky or feed him easily.

"I can come every day to walk and feed Lucky until you are able to do it yourself," suggested Raj.

"Thank you!" said Mrs. Brown. "We are both lucky that you are our friend!"

GO ON →

Use "Lucky" to answer Numbers 1 through 5.

1 **Circle** the word that tells what *portraits* are.

2 Why does Mrs. Brown need someone to care for Lucky?

_____

_____

3 **Underline** details that show how Mrs. Brown feels about putting Lucky in a kennel.

How does Raj help Mrs. Brown solve her problem?

_____

_____

4 **Circle** the clue that tells what Lucky does to *express* that he is happy.

What does *express* mean?

_____

_____

5 **Draw a box** around details that tell about Mrs. Brown's problem when she comes home from the hospital.

How does Raj help Mrs. Brown solve this problem?

_____

_____

STOP

Read "Johnny Appleseed" before you answer Numbers 1 through 5.

Johnny Appleseed

John Chapman was born in Massachusetts in 1774. Johnny left home at age eighteen. At this time, many people were heading west to build homes in new lands. Johnny wanted to travel to all these **settlements**. He wanted to plant apple trees so no one would be hungry. Each winter, Johnny collected sacks of apple seeds. Then he headed out on foot through the wilderness to plant the seeds in spring.

Johnny traveled hundreds and hundreds of miles each year. He was a strange sight because he usually walked barefoot! He wore a coffee sack with holes cut out for his head and arms and a tin cooking pot on his head. But no one **scoffed** or laughed at how he looked. Instead, they praised him for his efforts.

Johnny was a kind and gentle man who made friends with people and animals. Once he put out a campfire with his bare hands because the flames were harming insects!

Johnny walked for years and years. He planted thousands of apple trees. He gave away seeds for people to plant their own trees. So people gave him the nickname Johnny Appleseed. Some of the trees he planted still grow apples today.

GO ON →

Use "Johnny Appleseed" to answer Numbers 1 through 5.

1 Why does Johnny leave home at age eighteen?

_____

_____

Underline the details that tell what Johnny thinks will be the effect of his actions.

2 **Circle** the clues that tell the meaning of *settlements*.

What does *settlements* mean?

_____

3 What does Johnny do because of his kind nature?

_____

_____

Underline the details in the third paragraph that show Johnny is a larger-than-life character.

4 **Circle** a word that means almost the SAME as *scoffed*.

5 What nickname do people give John Chapman?

_____

Draw a box around the details that tell why he is given this nickname.

STOP

Read "James Naismith" before you answer Numbers 1 through 5.

James Naismith

When James Naismith was a boy, he liked to play games. He was a talented athlete. His **genuine** interest and real love for sports made him decide to be a gym teacher.

A New Game

Naismith taught physical education in Massachusetts. In the winter of 1891, it was too cold to exercise outdoors. He needed a new indoor game for his students to play, so he invented the game of basketball. He used a soccer ball and two peach baskets as goals. But the game was not perfect. Each time a player scored, someone had to climb a ladder to get the ball out of the basket.

A Changing Game

The game quickly became popular. Through the years, the baskets changed. Eventually, they became open hoops with nets like the ones still used **nowadays**. Some of the rules of the sport have changed, too. Today, basketball is one of the most popular sports in the world.

James Naismith's Time Line

1860	1885	1910	1935	1960
1861 Naismith is born in Ontario, Canada.		**1891** Naismith organizes the first basketball game.	**1939** Naismith dies in Kansas.	**1959** Naismith is included in the Basketball Hall of Fame.

GO ON →

Name: _____ Date: _____

Use "James Naismith" to answer Numbers 1 through 5.

1 **Circle** the clues that show that Naismith had a *genuine* interest in sports.

What does *genuine* mean?

_____

2 **Underline** the details that describe the problem Naismith had in the winter of 1891.

How did Naismith solve this problem?

_____

_____

3 **Underline** the details that describe the problem with using peach baskets as basketball nets.

How has this problem been solved over the years?

_____

4 **Circle** the clues that tell the meaning of *nowadays*.

What does *nowadays* mean?

_____

5 **Draw a box** around the event in the time line that shows a solution to a problem that Naismith had.

STOP

Read "A Look Inside" before you answer Numbers 1 through 5.

A Look Inside

An MRI is a special test that doctors use to see inside a patient's body. The test does not hurt at all. Doctors do an MRI test to look for any problems inside the body.

How It Works

An MRI scanner is a machine with a large magnet shaped like a tunnel. For each scan, a table slides in and out of the machine. First, a patient lies down on the table. Next, the table slides into the tunnel. The scanner sends painless magnet and radio waves inside the patient's body. After a few seconds, the information goes to a computer. The computer then creates pictures. Doctors look at all of the pictures on a computer screen. If they need a closer look, they can **magnify** a picture by making it larger on the screen.

MRI Technology

The first MRI test on a human was done in 1977. It took five hours to create just one picture. MRI machines have gotten better since then. Today, a **typical** or normal exam takes about one hour. It creates millions of pictures. The pictures help doctors see any problems inside the body. Doctors then decide the best way to treat their patients and make them healthy again.

GO ON →

Use "A Look Inside" to answer Numbers 1 through 5.

1 **Draw a box** around the signal words in the second paragraph that show an order of events.

What do the events tell about?

_____

2 **Circle** the clues that tell the meaning of *magnify*.

If you *magnify* something, is it easier or harder to see?

_____

3 **Underline** the event that happened in 1977.

How did the MRI test change AFTER 1977?

_____

_____

4 Write the word from the article that means almost the SAME as *typical*.

_____

5 What do doctors do AFTER looking at MRI pictures?

_____

_____

STOP

Read "Digging Up History" before you answer Numbers 1 through 5.

Digging Up History

Historic Find

In 2005, construction workers in San Francisco made an amazing discovery. Buried in the ground was part of an old ship. Two sperm-whale teeth were found in the ship. They were **evidence** that the ship was used to hunt whales. After studying old newspapers and ship records, scientists learned that the ship was the *Candace*, built in Boston around 1818.

History Uncovered

The *Candace* sailed for many years. During one whaling **expedition** to the Arctic, it was damaged by ice. On this trip, the ship barely made it back to San Francisco. Its final trip was in 1855.

Discovering the ship helped researchers learn about San Francisco's history. Between 1849 and 1856, people traveled there searching for gold. People traveled by ship, and many ships were left there. The site where the *Candace* was found was once a ship-breaking yard for these ships. Researchers believe the *Candace* was the last ship to be broken apart.

GO ON →

Use "Digging Up History" to answer Numbers 1 through 5.

1 **Draw a box** around the date when the *Candace* was discovered.

When was the *Candace* built?

_____

2 **Circle** the details that tell about the *evidence* that was found in the ship.

What does *evidence* mean?

_____

3 **Underline** the sentence that tells when the *Candace* sailed for the LAST time.

What do archaeologists think happened to the *Candace* AFTER its final voyage?

_____

_____

4 **Circle** a word that means almost the SAME as *expedition*.

What does *expedition* mean?

_____

5 **Draw a box** around the place on the map where people traveled between 1849 and 1856.

Read "Traditions, Old and New" before you answer Numbers 1 through 5.

Traditions, Old and New

Sarah rushed home from her job at her father's apron factory. She and her family lived on Orchard Street on the Lower East Side of New York City. They lived in a tiny apartment since arriving there in 1913.

"Hello, Mama," said Sarah as she opened the door.

"Oh, good, you are home," said Mother. "It is time to make *burekas*, so please prepare the crust and filling."

Sarah began rolling out the dough for the tiny pies. "Why do we eat burekas every Friday night?" asked Sarah.

"It is a tradition. Our family has always made burekas since your **ancestors**—my grandparents—made them in Greece. It is an **honor**. Our family shows respect by keeping this tradition."

"Can we make a new tradition?" asked Sarah. She had been saving pennies that she earned from work.

"What would you like to do?" Mother asked.

Sarah wanted to treat her brothers to the moving picture show. It could be their monthly tradition. The boys loved Charlie Chaplin best. The show was only five cents.

Mother hugged Sarah. "You are a good girl, Sarah. That will be a nice tradition to start."

GO ON →

Use "Traditions, Old and New" to answer Numbers 1 through 5.

1 **Underline** the details that tell about Sarah's family tradition on Friday nights.

Why do they keep this tradition?

_____

_____

2 **Circle** the details that tell who Sarah's *ancestors* are.

What does *ancestors* mean?

_____

_____

3 **Circle** the clues that show why it is an *honor* for Sarah's family to make burekas.

What does *honor* mean?

_____

_____

4 **Draw a box** around the details that describe a new tradition Sarah would like to start.

5 How does Sarah's mother feel about Sarah's idea for a new tradition?

_____

Underline the details that support your answer.

_____

Read "History in 2003" before you answer Numbers 1 through 5.

History in 2003

"In 1903, students buried a time capsule that Principal Murray opened this morning in honor of its 100-year anniversary," explained Mrs. Sanchez.

Mara asked, "What will we learn from 100 years ago?"

"Each student wrote an essay that **depicts**, or describes, experiences they had and wanted to share with future children. Many were from faraway countries, and they passed through Ellis Island on their way to America."

Mrs. Sanchez read an essay by a boy from Italy.

*We waited nervously in the Great Room until the medical exam when the doctor lifted up our eyelids. Everyone **detested** this awful exam! The doctor wanted to see if we had an eye infection. Thank goodness, my family passed the test, and we did not have to return to Italy!*

My family was asked many questions, such as Where were you born? *and* Where are you going to live? *Afterward, we went downstairs to the Kissing Post.*

"What is the Kissing Post?" laughed another student.

Mrs. Sanchez continued reading.

Uncle Carlo waited for us in this room. We ran to him, kissed, and sighed with relief because we were now in America.

GO ON →

Use "History in 2003" to answer Numbers 1 through 5.

1 **Circle** the word that restates what *depicts* means.

2 **Underline** the details that tell why the boy's family is nervous.

3 **Circle** the clues that show what *detested* means.

What does *detested* mean?

_____

4 **Draw a box** around the details that tell about the Kissing Post.

How did the Kissing Post get its name?

_____

_____

5 Tell how a time capsule is an important record from the past.

_____

_____

STOP

Read "Fire for Energy" before you answer Numbers 1 through 5.

Fire for Energy

I often wonder how people survived long ago when they did not have modern things, such as electricity and gas. Think about sitting in a dark cave, huddled under an animal hide—shivering through the night! Imagine not being able to sit in your heated home at night, using a light to read a book.

The first kind of energy people used was the sun. It provided both light and heat and was a **renewable** energy source that never ran out. However, once the sun set, people headed for caves, seeking shelter from the cold. There was no electricity in caves. People used the moon and stars for light and animal hides for warmth.

We do not know exactly when humans began lighting fires. During thunderstorms, they may have seen lightning strike trees. Perhaps they saw the fire and felt its warmth. Someone carried a burning branch to a cave. They added branches to the fire to keep it lit. People **converted**, or changed, wood into an energy source. From there, they built their own fires and discovered that fire cooked food and helped them make tools for hunting. How life-changing fire must have been! It helped many people survive long ago.

GO ON →

Name: _____ Date: _____

Use "Fire for Energy" to answer Numbers 1 through 5.

1 **Underline** key details that describe what life was like long ago.

2 **Circle** the clues that show how the sun is a *renewable* energy source.

What does *renewable* mean?

_____

_____

3 Tell how people may have first started using fire.

_____

_____

_____

4 **Circle** the word that tells the meaning of *converted*.

5 Why was it important that people started using fire as an energy source?

_____

_____

_____

Draw a box around the details that support your answer.

STOP

Read "How Paper Money Is Made" before you answer Numbers 1 through 5.

How Paper Money Is Made

Each time you give money to buy something, a **transaction** takes place. All business transactions require **currency**, or money. Paper bills are one type of currency. They are produced at the Bureau of Engraving and Printing in Washington, D.C. and in Texas.

Making Paper Money

Have you looked closely at a dollar bill and noticed its detail? Each bill has a design and code that identify it. Many steps go into making paper money. It is first designed, and then the design is put onto printing plates. One plate might include a background pattern. Another plate might include different colored pictures and writing.

Blank sheets of paper then pass through a machine called a printing press. This machine prints the background colors and images onto the paper. After it dries, the paper is laid on top of another plate and pressed together. This helps to form a finished image on the money.

From the Printing Press to You

Finally, the money is wrapped in plastic and stored in a vault. The Federal Reserve Bank gives them to banks, which then distribute them to you.

GO ON →

Use "How Paper Money Is Made" to answer Numbers 1 through 5.

1 **Circle** the clues that tell the meaning of *transaction*.

What does *transaction* mean?

_____

_____

2 **Circle** an example of *currency*.

What is the meaning of *currency*?

_____

_____

3 **Underline** the key detail that tells how bills are identified.

4 What role does the printing press have in making money?

_____

_____

5 **Draw a box** around the section that tells what happens *after* money is printed.

What is the MAIN idea of this section?

_____

_____

STOP

Read "Me, Myself, and Dad" before you answer Numbers 1 through 5.

Me, Myself, and Dad

Mom says "Slow down!" when we gobble dinner—

quick as a flash, the pasta and salad are gone!

We are both "lefties," while Mom and Sis are not.

We both have a silly sense of humor:

Who has a good "Knock, Knock" joke today?

On Sundays, we have a tradition of watching football.

We pop the popcorn, slip on our blue jerseys,

sit on the couch, our left ankle crossed over right.

We love to read biographies of great people in history:

Jackie Robinson and Martin Luther King, Jr.

But sometimes, I'm just me:

Unique, an individual, and one of a kind—

with my own set of roots growing deep and wide—

introducing me to new people, places, and things.

I can play sports well, while he has two left feet.

My voice is sharp and high-pitched:

His is deep, gentle, and low.

But maybe I will change as I grow older.

Who knows?

For now, it's me, myself, and Dad!

GO ON →

Use "Me, Myself, and Dad" to answer Numbers 1 through 5.

1 **Draw a box** around the details in the *first* stanza that tell how the narrator and his dad are ALIKE.

2 How do the narrator and his dad look when they watch football?

_____

_____

Underline the details that help you picture them watching a game.

3 **Circle** the details that compare the narrator's roots to a person.

4 **Underline** the details that tell how the narrator is DIFFERENT from his dad.

How does the narrator feel about being *different* from his dad?

_____

_____

5 Tell one reason why this is a free verse poem.

_____

_____

STOP

Mid-Unit Assessment

Read "The Prince's Wish" before you answer Numbers 1 through 5.

The Prince's Wish

You couldn't tell just by looking, but James was not like other children. He was a prince. One day, he would be king.

A prince might sound like a wonderful thing to be, but James wanted to be a normal boy. He did not want to wear fine clothes. Nor did he want to sit on a throne for hours, listening to **official** speeches about the state of the kingdom. He loved his parents, but sometimes he wished they were farmers.

One morning, James was looking out his window in the castle. He sighed as he watched children playing in the courtyard below.

"I wish I was a normal boy," he said.

Suddenly, he heard a noise behind him. A blur of color filled the castle tower. The color faded and a young girl appeared. She wore a white gown and held a sparkling wand.

"Who are you?" James asked.

"A fairy princess," she answered.

James frowned. "But you are young like me. Shouldn't you be playing with the other children? Or home with your family?"

GO ON →

The girl nodded sadly. "I should have waited until I was older, but I left home against my parents' wishes. Now, I cannot find my way back."

James did not know what to say. "Why are you here?" he finally asked.

"To grant your wish."

He straightened, excited. "Can you make me a normal boy?"

"Yes," the girl said. "But you will have to leave home."

"Can my parents come with me?" James asked.

"No," she answered. "You will have to leave them, too. You'll be just like me."

James looked out the window again. His parents were walking through the gardens. His mother, the queen, waved when she saw him.

James turned to the girl. "I'm ready to make my wish," he declared.

The girl held up her wand.

"I wish," James said, "that you can go back home."

The girl's eyes widened. "Thank you," she whispered softly. Then she disappeared.

James smiled and ran to join his parents.

GO ON →

Use "The Prince's Wish" to answer Numbers 1 through 5.

1 Read these sentences from the passage.

> Nor did he want to sit on a throne for hours, listening to official speeches about the state of the kingdom. He loved his parents, but sometimes he wished they were farmers.

Which evidence from the sentences helps to explain the meaning of *official*?

Ⓐ sit on a throne for hours

Ⓑ speeches about the state of the kingdom

Ⓒ he wished they were farmers

2 What is James doing when the girl appears?

Ⓐ sitting on a throne

Ⓑ waving to his mother

Ⓒ watching children play

3 What problem does the girl have?

Ⓐ She cannot grant wishes.

Ⓑ She wants to be a princess.

Ⓒ She cannot find her way home.

GO ON →

4 How does James help the girl solve her problem?

Ⓐ He makes a wish for her.

Ⓑ He shows her the way home.

Ⓒ He invites her to live in the castle.

5 What does James do AFTER the girl disappears?

Ⓐ He goes to be with his parents.

Ⓑ He joins the children who are playing.

Ⓒ He tries to find out where the girl went.

Read "Tornadoes: Dangerous Weather" before you answer Numbers 6 through 10.

Tornadoes: Dangerous Weather

You look up into the sky. A dark cloud stretches to the ground. That cloud is a tornado. A tornado has strong winds that can lift up cars. They can destroy buildings. A tornado can cause a natural disaster in seconds.

Tornado Features

Tornadoes can happen almost anywhere. They form on land or water. Most tornadoes happen in the United States.

Like thunderstorms, most tornadoes occur in the spring and summer. They can form when winds in a thunderstorm change direction. The winds begin turning. They pick up speed. Soon they rise up to form a funnel. The funnel is a tube-shaped cloud.

Most tornadoes have wind speeds of about 110 miles an hour. The strongest tornadoes have wind speeds up to 200 miles an hour. Tornadoes can last less than a minute. They can also last more than an hour.

All tornadoes form quickly. Their paths are **unpredictable.** No one is certain about where they will go. Tornadoes can destroy one area. They can leave the next area unharmed.

GO ON →

Be Prepared

You can stay safe if a tornado hits. Go inside at the first sign of a storm. Listen to the news. If a tornado is on the way, go to the basement. You can also go to a room without windows.

Keep an emergency kit on hand. Always be prepared for a weather-related danger or **hazard**.

How Tornadoes Form

Winds change direction and speed. They begin to spin.

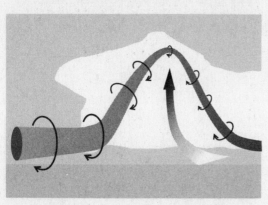

The spinning winds rise upward.

The funnel stretches from the cloud to the ground.

GO ON →

Use "Tornadoes: Dangerous Weather" to answer Numbers 6 through 10.

6 According to the article, what do thunderstorms and tornadoes have in common?

Ⓐ Both are difficult to predict.

Ⓑ Both occur mainly in spring and summer.

Ⓒ Both have wind speeds up to 200 miles an hour.

7 Read this paragraph from the article.

> All tornadoes form quickly. Their paths are unpredictable. No one is certain about where they will go. Tornadoes can destroy one area. They can leave the next area unharmed.

Which word from the paragraph means the OPPOSITE of *unpredictable*?

Ⓐ certain

Ⓑ destroy

Ⓒ unharmed

8 How are all tornadoes ALIKE?

Ⓐ They form quickly.

Ⓑ They form on land.

Ⓒ They follow the same path.

GO ON →

9 Read this paragraph from the article.

> **Keep an emergency kit on hand. Always be prepared for a weather-related danger or hazard.**

Which word from the paragraph has about the SAME meaning as *hazard*?

Ⓐ emergency

Ⓑ prepared

Ⓒ danger

10 According to the diagram, what is the FIRST stage in the formation of a tornado?

Ⓐ The spinning winds rise up.

Ⓑ The funnel touches the ground.

Ⓒ The winds change direction and speed.

STOP

Read "The Crows Are in the Corn" before you answer Numbers 1 through 5.

The Crows Are in the Corn

One beautiful day in Georgia, a farmer and his wife wanted to sleep late. They were hardworking people every other day. But on this day, they wanted to feel rich. So, they slept all morning long. The sun outside was **dazzling** and bright, but the farmer and his wife just kept sleeping.

Along came a gathering of crows. The crows spotted the quiet house and the lack of people to chase them away. Then they saw the golden corn in the field.

Now, crows like corn. Everyone knows that. And this corn was ready to eat.

"Caw, caw!" the crows cackled. They dived down for the ripe, delicious corn.

The noise woke up the old rooster.

"Wake up! Wake up!" he clucked to the sleeping farmer and his wife. But nothing would wake them.

The farmer and his wife just rolled over in bed and kept on sleeping.

"Caw, caw!" the crows called as they crunched on the juicy corn.

The rooster became **annoyed** with the farmer and his wife. Now he was bothered. They just would not listen to him.

GO ON →

So he called again, louder this time. "The crows are in the corn! The crows are in the corn!"

But the farmer and his wife just kept sleeping. The farmer snored louder and his wife put the pillow over her head.

The rooster panicked. He called in his loudest pitch. "The crows are pulling up the corn!"

But the farmer and his wife did not wake up. Meanwhile, the crows kept eating and eating.

The rooster finally gave up. He could not wake them. The crows finished eating all the corn in the field. The farmer and his wife finally woke up and looked outside. They saw that all the corn was gone.

To this day in Georgia, when they say, "The crows are in the corn," it is time to get up!

GO ON →

Use "The Crows Are in the Corn" to answer Numbers 1 through 5.

1 Read these sentences from the passage.

> But on this day, they wanted to feel rich. So, they slept all morning long. The sun outside was dazzling and bright, but the farmer and his wife just kept sleeping.

Which word from these sentences has about the SAME meaning as *dazzling*?

Ⓐ rich

Ⓑ long

Ⓒ bright

2 What evidence from the text tells why the crows dived into the field?

Ⓐ And this corn was ready to eat.

Ⓑ The noise woke up the old rooster.

Ⓒ But nothing would wake them.

3 Read this sentence from the passage.

The rooster became annoyed with the farmer and his wife.

Which sentence from the passage gives a clue about the meaning of *annoyed*?

Ⓐ Now, crows like corn.

Ⓑ Now he was bothered.

Ⓒ So he called again, louder this time.

4 Why does the rooster keep calling to the farmer and his wife?

Ⓐ They are sleeping late and missing a beautiful morning.

Ⓑ The crows are making too much noise in the fields.

Ⓒ They need to wake up to chase away the crows.

5 What is the overall message of this passage?

Ⓐ It is important to pay attention to your responsibilities.

Ⓑ People should not ignore advice from others.

Ⓒ Farm animals can be helpful to their owners.

Read "The Everglades" before you answer Numbers 6 through 10.

The Everglades

Sally lives in southern Florida. She lives near an area called the Everglades. The area is very large. It is 100 miles long and 50 miles wide. It looks like a sea of grass. One day, a forest ranger visited her school. She told Sally's class about the Everglades.

A Perfect Balance

The Everglades are part of a wetlands ecosystem. Wetlands have a special kind of soil. When it rains, the soil absorbs the water. The soil acts like a sponge. This prevents the area from flooding. When it is dry, the soil slowly releases the water. This helps keep the land wet and also prevents **droughts**, or very dry conditions.

An Ecosystem at Risk

The Everglades are in danger now. Years ago, people thought the swampy land was useless. They wanted to build on the land and use it for farming. So, they drained the land. Water from the wetlands went into the ocean. This changed the Everglades. Eventually, water from the farms flowed back into the wetlands. Water flowed in from nearby cities. Sometimes the water was polluted or dirty.

GO ON →

Once the Everglades had many different plants and animals. But with less water, plants and animals had problems. There wasn't enough clean water for the plants. Plants began to die. But, animals needed the plants to live. Sometimes they could not find food. Some animals died or left. Now the area has fewer plants and animals.

The forest ranger said people are affected by changes to the Everglades. They worry about flooding, droughts, and their drinking water. People are working to save the Everglades. Sally wants to help, too.

Water in the Everglades

> Clean water

> Healthy plants

> Healthy animals

GO ON →

Use "The Everglades" to answer Numbers 6 through 10.

6 Which phrase from the article gives a clue about the meaning of *droughts*?

Ⓐ special kind of soil

Ⓑ acts like a sponge

Ⓒ very dry conditions

7 Which sentence from the article supports the idea that the wetlands are helpful?

Ⓐ The Everglades are part of a wetlands ecosystem.

Ⓑ When it is dry, the soil slowly releases the water.

Ⓒ The Everglades are in danger now.

8 Why did people drain the Everglades?

Ⓐ They wanted to use the land for other things.

Ⓑ They thought the swampy land was useful.

Ⓒ They needed more clean drinking water.

GO ON →

9 What is the MOST important idea that the flow chart shows?

Ⓐ Clean water is good for animals.

Ⓑ Both plants and animals need clean water.

Ⓒ The Everglades are made up of plants, animals, and water.

10 What is the MAIN idea of this article?

Ⓐ The Everglades is part of a wetlands ecosystem.

Ⓑ The Everglades is important to southern Florida.

Ⓒ The Everglades has many different types of animals.

STOP

Read "A Delicious Idea" before you answer Numbers 1 through 5.

A Delicious Idea

Shawna and her mom were standing at the kitchen counter. They were preparing a salad.

"I miss growing my own food," her mom said.

"You grew your own food?" Shawna asked.

Her mom nodded. "We had a garden when I was your age. I liked planting the seeds and watering the plants. I didn't even mind pulling weeds. And the vegetables we grew were delicious. It was such fun!"

At school the next morning, Shawna was still thinking about her mother's words. She stared out the window at the grass in the schoolyard. Shawna perked up when she heard the project their teacher was giving the class.

"I want you to work together to think of a way to help our community," Mr. Gomez said.

Shawna walked over to her friend Fran. "Let's plant a garden in the schoolyard," she suggested.

"What will we do with the food we grow?" Fran asked.

"We'll give it to people in need in the community. And we'll eat the rest!" Shawna said.

The girls told Mr. Gomez about their idea. He liked it, but he had some questions.

GO ON →

"Do you have gardening equipment? Do you have seeds? Do you have permission to dig up the schoolyard?" Mr. Gomez asked.

Shawna and Fran had a lot of work to do! First, they got permission from their principal. Then, a construction worker helped them plow the soil. A gardening store donated seeds. The store gave seeds for vegetables that were **complementary**, or would grow well together in the garden. A hardware store loaned them gardening tools.

Together, they **gingerly** planted the tiny seeds, making sure to be very careful. They grew squash, tomatoes, and lettuce. Within months, they were handing out pounds of fresh vegetables! Shawna and Fran got an "A" on the project. That made Shawna happy, but not as happy as hearing her mother's words.

"How delicious!" her mom said as she ate the freshest salad she had tasted in years.

GO ON →

Use "A Delicious Idea" to answer Numbers 1 through 5.

1 Who is the narrator of the passage?

Ⓐ a speaker not in the story

Ⓑ Shawna's mom

Ⓒ Shawna

2 Which text evidence shows what Shawna's mom thinks about having her own garden?

Ⓐ They were preparing a salad.

Ⓑ "We had a garden when I was your age."

Ⓒ "It was such fun!"

3 Read this sentence from the passage.

> **The store gave seeds for vegetables that were complementary, or would grow well together in the garden.**

Which words from the sentence give a clue about the meaning of *complementary*?

Ⓐ seeds for vegetables

Ⓑ grow well together

Ⓒ in the garden

4 Read this sentence from the passage.

> **Together, they gingerly planted the tiny seeds, making sure to be very careful.**

Which word from the sentence helps to explain the meaning of *gingerly*?

Ⓐ together

Ⓑ tiny

Ⓒ careful

5 What does Shawna think about the results of her project at the end of the passage?

Ⓐ She thinks her garden is better than her mom's garden.

Ⓑ She is happy and proud of the garden she grew.

Ⓒ She wants to grow another garden at home.

GO ON →

Read "Helen Keller" before you answer Numbers 6 through 10.

Helen Keller

Helen Keller worked all her life for the rights of people who were blind and deaf. She understood the challenges they faced because she was blind and deaf, too.

Early Life

Helen was born in 1880 in Alabama. She was a smart baby. She spoke her first words at only six months old. She could see and hear then. When Helen was 19 months, she had a high fever. Helen recovered from the fever, but she had changed. She did not follow people with her eyes now. She did not jump if there was a loud sound. Helen could no longer see or hear.

Helen and Anne

By the age of seven, Helen had become an angry girl. She was out of control. Losing hope, Helen's mother hired a teacher to help her daughter. The teacher was Anne Sullivan. Helen was stubborn, but Anne was, too. Anne would not give up.

One day, Anne held Helen's hand under running water. She spelled the letters W-A-T-E-R in her palm. Helen's face lit up. She finally understood that letters spell out words and that words stand for objects. Her world changed.

GO ON →

Making a Difference

Helen learned 30 more words that day. She went on to learn five languages! With Anne by her side, she went to college. She wrote 11 books and worked to help others **fulfill,** or reach, their dreams. She traveled to many countries, educating people about the deaf and blind. She died in 1968. Helen Keller changed our view forever of the deaf and blind.

The Life of Helen Keller

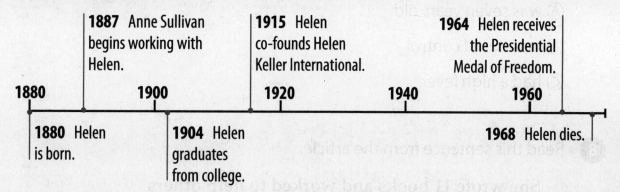

Name: _____ Date: _____

Use "Helen Keller" to answer Numbers 6 through 10.

6 What evidence from the text supports the author's point of view that Helen was a smart baby?

Ⓐ She spoke her first words at only six months old.

Ⓑ She could see and hear then.

Ⓒ She did not jump if there was a loud sound.

7 The author describes Helen's mother as losing hope because Helen _____.

Ⓐ was seven years old

Ⓑ was out of control

Ⓒ had a high fever

8 Read this sentence from the article.

> **She wrote 11 books and worked to help others fulfill, or reach, their dreams.**

Which clue word from the sentence helps to explain what *fulfill* means?

Ⓐ wrote

Ⓑ help

Ⓒ reach

GO ON →

94 Grade 4   **Mid-Unit Assessment · Unit 3**

Copyright © McGraw-Hill Education. Permission is granted to reproduce for classroom use.

9 What does the author MOST LIKELY think about the day that Anne taught Helen the word *water*?

Ⓐ Helen's life would change from this event.

Ⓑ Helen's teacher would always stay with her.

Ⓒ Helen would learn to see and hear one day.

10 Based on the time line, what major event took place in Helen's life not long before she died?

Ⓐ She received the Presidential Medal of Freedom.

Ⓑ She created Helen Keller International.

Ⓒ She graduated from college.

STOP

Read "Planet Zeno" before you answer Numbers 1 through 5.

Planet Zeno

Jack's family had come to live on planet Zeno. It was exciting to be living on a new planet among different people. Soon Jack started his new school. The other students were friendly, and many of them also came from different planets. Jack decided to run for Student Planet Council President. He started asking other kids in school if they would vote for him.

First, he met a girl from the faraway planet of Viston. She wore two pairs of eyeglasses because she had eyes in the front and back of her head. He asked if she would vote for him.

"It would be a **privilege**. I would be honored," she replied. "Will the Council give everyone free glasses?"

"What if they can't?" asked Jack.

"Then just be fair. That's all that really counts," she smiled.

Next, Jack met a boy from Aquos. His planet was made up of water. He was breathing from a tall pitcher of water.

"Will you vote for me for Council?" asked Jack.

"I'll vote for you if the Council gives everyone new pitchers each year."

"What if they can't?" asked Jack.

GO ON →

"Well, just treat everyone with respect," he replied. Then he waved goodbye.

Jack went into the lunchroom. He met a boy wearing a heated solar suit. He was from a very cold planet called Arcon. Jack asked the boy if he would vote for him.

"Sure. I'll vote for you if the Council can repair my suit when it breaks," he said.

"And if they can't?" asked Jack.

The boy thought for a minute. "In that case, just be sure the Council is honest." Then he reached out from his solar suit and shook Jack's hand.

Jack felt glad as he thought about the students he had met. Did they all **intend,** or plan, to vote for him? Each student wanted something different. But they had something in common. They all agreed that fairness, respect, and honesty were most important. These things were important to Jack, too. He would run the council on these principles. He knew he could earn their votes this way.

GO ON →

Use "Planet Zeno" to answer Numbers 1 through 5.

1 Who is the narrator of the passage?

   Ⓐ Jack

   Ⓑ a speaker not in the story

   Ⓒ the Student Planet Council President

2 Read this paragraph from the passage.

> **"It would be a privilege. I would be honored," she replied. "Will the Council give everyone free glasses?"**

Which word from the paragraph has about the SAME meaning as *privilege*?

   Ⓐ honored

   Ⓑ replied

   Ⓒ free

3 Which sentence from the passage shows what the boy from Aquos thinks about Jack as Council President?

   Ⓐ His planet was made up of water.

   Ⓑ "Will you vote for me for Council?" asked Jack.

   Ⓒ "Well, just treat everyone with respect," he replied.

GO ON →

4 Which word from the passage has about the SAME meaning as *intend*?

Ⓐ met

Ⓑ plan

Ⓒ agreed

5 What evidence from the text tells why Jack thinks he can earn students' votes?

Ⓐ He makes friends with many different students.

Ⓑ He decides to run for Student Planet Council President.

Ⓒ He will run the Council in a way that benefits everyone.

GO ON →

Read "The Map" before you answer Numbers 6 through 10.

The Map

"Hey, Dad, look what I found in the attic," said Alex as he held out a map. "It sure looks complicated."

"That is a map of the old highway system. See, it's dated 1918. People could finally afford to buy cars, so they wanted to drive places."

"What was it like back then?"

"Well, that was before I was born, but I know driving was difficult. City roads were all right, but country roads were terrible. Many were dirt or gravel. You couldn't drive far before getting stuck in the mud or getting a flat tire."

"That doesn't sound like fun."

"People usually like an adventure, and some people wanted to drive across the country. The most popular road was the Lincoln Highway. It went from New York City to San Francisco. In 1918, the trip took 20 to 30 days, and some trucks took months to cross the country."

"Why did it take so long?"

"The roads were bad and the maps were hard to follow. The route was made up of many smaller roads that didn't connect to each other. The map showed how to get from one road to another. Each route had a different color. People put up colored signs on posts and telephone poles, **directing** traffic. That way, drivers could follow the route. Soon, people wanted better roads."

GO ON →

"I bet they did," said Alex. "What happened next?"

Alex's dad went on to explain how the roads improved over time. Around 1956, the President had a plan. The President's name was Eisenhower. People called him Ike. Ike thought good roads would make the country stronger. His plan was called the Interstate (IN•tur•state) Highway System. The project took almost forty years to complete. As a result, people can now drive across the country in five days.

"Ike was right. The interstate makes travel easier. We take it to get to the ballpark," said Alex.

Alex's dad nodded. "I've got an idea. Let's get on the interstate. I feel like having an adventure!"

GO ON →

Use "The Map" to answer Numbers 6 through 10.

6 Which of the following was NOT an effect of the old highway system?

Ⓐ Cars got stuck in the mud or got flat tires.

Ⓑ People only wanted to drive on city roads.

Ⓒ It took some trucks months to cross the country.

7 Read this sentence from the passage.

> His plan was called the Interstate (IN•tur•state) Highway System.

What is the purpose of the letters in parentheses?

Ⓐ to show how to pronounce the word

Ⓑ to teach the meaning of the word

Ⓑ to help spell the word

8 Why did Ike want to make the Interstate Highway System?

Ⓐ He thought good roads would make the country stronger.

Ⓑ He thought people wanted to have an adventure.

Ⓒ He thought maps were too confusing.

GO ON →

9 Read these sentences from the passage.

> **"People put up colored signs on posts and telephone poles, directing traffic. That way, drivers could follow the route."**

Which phrase from the sentences gives a clue about the meaning of *directing*?

Ⓐ on posts

Ⓑ telephone poles

Ⓒ follow the route

10 Which sentence from the text signals a cause-and-effect relationship?

Ⓐ The map showed how to get from one road to another.

Ⓑ Alex's dad went on to explain how the roads improved over time.

Ⓒ As a result, people can now drive across the country in five days.

STOP

Read "Short Cut Sam" before you answer Numbers 1 through 5.

Short Cut Sam

Short Cut Sam was a Pony Express rider. He rode hundreds of miles to deliver the mail. Short Cut would ride those horses as fast as he could. He would run across the wild prairies of the West.

Short Cut got his nickname because he was the youngest and smallest Pony Express rider. The older riders liked to joke with him, especially Long Leg Jim and Bronco Bob.

"Here comes Short Cut," Jim would holler.

"Where?" Bob hollered back. All the while, Short Cut stood right in front of them.

Short Cut didn't like this very much. One day, he came up with a plan. He knew that if he could prove he was the fastest rider, no one would ever tease him again.

"Hey, Jim. I bet I can beat you to California," he challenged.

Jim laughed. "Is that so? All right. But if I win, I get your horse, Windy."

Short Cut hesitated. Windy was his favorite horse. She was also his best friend.

"Scared?" Jim teased.

"No!" Short Cut insisted. But he was.

GO ON →

They raced the next day. With a wave of a flag, they were off!

Jim led from the start. Short Cut was close behind. They raced all through the day and all through the night. They didn't even stop to eat. Short Cut rode so fast that Windy's iron horseshoes nearly melted!

Short Cut saw Jim stop up ahead. A huge canyon lay before them. It was a mile wide and a mile deep. Jim galloped away. He looked for a way around it. Short Cut lowered his head to Windy's ear.

"Let's jump it, girl," he whispered.

Windy reared up on her hind legs. They were off! They picked up speed. With one mighty leap, they jumped the canyon. For minutes, they hung in the air. In a great **whirl** of spinning dust, they landed safely on the other side.

You can probably guess what happened next. Short Cut reached California first. People still called him Short Cut after that. His short cut had earned him the title of the greatest rider in the West.

GO ON →

Use "Short Cut Sam" to answer Numbers 1 through 5.

1 What problem does Short Cut have at the beginning of the passage?

Ⓐ He is teased by the other Pony Express riders.

Ⓑ He is not old enough to be a Pony Express rider.

Ⓒ He is too small to ride the horses in the Pony Express.

2 How does Short Cut solve his problem?

Ⓐ He buys a new horse.

Ⓑ He proves he is the fastest rider.

Ⓒ He asks the other riders for help.

3 What causes Long Leg Jim to stop during the race?

Ⓐ He is hungry and needs to eat.

Ⓑ He comes to a wide, deep canyon.

Ⓒ He thinks he has reached California.

GO ON →

4 Read this sentence from the passage.

> **In a great whirl of spinning dust, they landed safely on the other side.**

Which clue words from the sentence help to explain what *whirl* means?

Ⓐ spinning dust

Ⓑ landed safely

Ⓒ other side

5 How does Short Cut get to California before Jim?

Ⓐ He finds a new horse.

Ⓑ He jumps the canyon.

Ⓒ He rides through the night.

Read "A Better Bag" before you answer Numbers 6 through 10.

A Better Bag

Even as a young girl, Margaret Knight was a great problem solver. In 1850, she made her first invention. She saw a worker at a plant get hurt when a thread caught on a machine. Margaret made a special device. It stopped the machine when any problems arose. She was 12 years old.

A Practical Invention

Margaret invented many things. She is best known for making a better paper bag. In 1868, she was working at a paper bag plant. Paper bags were like envelopes back then. They could not stand up. They would **topple** over.

Margaret came up with a machine that made paper bags with flat bottoms. These new bags could be filled easily. They could also stand up.

Margaret wanted to get a patent for her invention. However, her hopes almost **withered,** or died, away. A man named Charles Annan claimed that he had made the machine.

The case went to court. Annan said that no woman could have come up with such a good idea. He lost his case and Margaret got her patent in 1871.

GO ON →

A Great Inventor

Margaret started the Eastern Paper Bag Company to make her bags. She received more than 20 different patents during her life. She died in 1914.

Walk into any grocery store or shopping mall today. You will see Margaret's flat-bottom bags still being used!

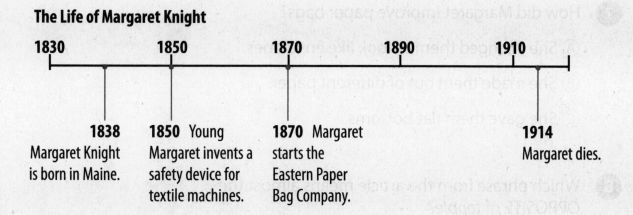

The Life of Margaret Knight

| 1830 | 1850 | 1870 | 1890 | 1910 |

1838 Margaret Knight is born in Maine.

1850 Young Margaret invents a safety device for textile machines.

1870 Margaret starts the Eastern Paper Bag Company.

1914 Margaret dies.

GO ON →

Use "A Better Bag" to answer Numbers 6 through 10.

6 What problem caused Margaret to make her first invention when she was 12 years old?

Ⓐ People said women did not have good ideas.

Ⓑ Paper bags would not stand upright.

Ⓒ A worker was hurt by a machine.

7 How did Margaret improve paper bags?

Ⓐ She changed them to look like envelopes.

Ⓑ She made them out of different paper.

Ⓒ She gave them flat bottoms.

8 Which phrase from the article means almost the OPPOSITE of *topple*?

Ⓐ stand upright

Ⓑ came up with

Ⓒ paper bags

GO ON →

9 Read this paragraph from the article.

> **Margaret wanted to get a patent for her invention. However, her hopes almost withered, or died, away. A man named Charles Annan claimed he had made the machine.**

Which word from the paragraph has about the SAME meaning as *withered*?

Ⓐ wanted

Ⓑ died

Ⓒ claimed

10 According to the time line, in what year did Margaret start the Eastern Paper Bag Company?

Ⓐ 1850

Ⓑ 1870

Ⓒ 1914

STOP

Read "The Storytellers" before you answer Numbers 1 through 5.

The Storytellers

It was the 1930s in America, and Rachel's family had a tradition. Every night, the whole family gathered in the parlor. They sat and listened to the nightly radio program together. Afterward, they would talk about the episode. Soon, everyone would start sharing stories about their past adventures.

The family loved the "Tarzan" program best. In the make-believe story, young Tarzan gets lost in a rainforest. Apes find him and raise him as their own. They teach him how to swim and swing from trees.

The program reminded Rachel's Uncle Merle of a story from his youth. As a boy, **obedience** was not in his nature. He did not always listen to his mother. She told him to stay away from the swimming hole. But he went there anyway. A little girl fell into the water. Merle rescued the girl. That little girl grew up to become the brave and fearless airplane pilot, Amelia Earhart! Amelia showed great **endurance** and strength. Only a few years ago she had become the first woman to fly across the Atlantic Ocean alone!

Aunt Celia shot Uncle Merle a suspecting look. "Oh, Merle! You saved the life of Amelia Earhart? That is rather unlikely."

Merle insisted it was true. Deep down, Rachel knew Uncle Merle was being truthful.

GO ON →

Another family favorite was "The Air Adventures of Jimmie Allen." The program featured the exciting adventures of young pilot, Jimmie. He flew around the world solving crimes.

Again, Uncle Merle had a story to share. He remembered his days in the Air Service as a young man. He flew some of the first airplanes. One day, he met a young pilot named Charles Lindbergh. Lindbergh did not have much money. He was not sure if he would continue flying. Merle talked him into remaining a pilot. Lindbergh went on to become one of the most famous pilots of his time!

Again, some family members had their doubts. They did not like made-up memories.

But the stories inspired Rachel. She did not care whether they really happened. The stories made her dream of having her own adventures one day. And maybe she would grow up to become a wonderful storyteller, just like her uncle!

GO ON →

Use "The Storytellers" to answer Numbers 1 through 5.

1 Read this sentence from the passage.

> **As a boy, obedience was not in his nature.**

Which sentence from the passage gives a clue about the meaning of *obedience*?

Ⓐ He did not always listen to his mother.

Ⓑ She told him to stay away from the swimming hole.

Ⓒ A little girl fell into the water.

2 Read these sentences from the passage.

> **Amelia showed great endurance and strength.**
> **Only a few years ago she had become the first**
> **woman to fly across the Atlantic Ocean alone.**

Which phrase from the sentences helps to explain what *endurance* means?

Ⓐ only a few years ago

Ⓑ the first woman

Ⓒ fly across the Atlantic Ocean

GO ON →

3 What would Aunt Celia probably say about Uncle Merle's stories?

Ⓐ Not all stories people tell are actually true.

Ⓑ Stories from the past teach important lessons.

Ⓒ Radio programs remind people of the best stories.

4 How does Rachel feel about Uncle Merle's stories?

Ⓐ She thinks they are probably not true.

Ⓑ She uses them to teach lessons about life.

Ⓒ She is inspired to live and tell stories of her own.

5 What is an overall message of this passage?

Ⓐ Not all stories about adventures are true.

Ⓑ Traditions can connect young and old people.

Ⓒ People can find adventures in their own backyards.

GO ON →

Read "The Solar Farm" before you answer Numbers 6 through 10.

The Solar Farm

Pat's class is studying energy resources. They learned that some resources are renewable, like the sun and wind. People will not use up these resources.

Today they are visiting a solar farm where they will learn how the sun is used to create electricity.

The bus arrived at the farm. Pat expected to see fields of corn, but instead she saw rows and rows of shiny panels! They were tilted up to face the sun.

Pat's teacher introduced Mr. Thomas. "Mr. Thomas is an engineer," she said. "He will teach us more about solar energy."

"Welcome, class," said Mr. Thomas. "I'm glad you came today. This solar farm is built on an old farm, but others are in different kinds of places. Some are on old parking lots. Some are on unused land. The best place is where there is no better use for the land."

George asked a question. "How does a solar farm work, Mr. Thomas?"

"Come with me," he said.

The class followed Mr. Thomas into the field.

GO ON →

"Look at the solar panels. Each one is at least as tall as you are! See how the panels are **installed,** or placed, so they turn toward the sun? When the sun shines, the panels collect the sun's energy. The panels turn the sun's energy into electricity. This electricity heats many homes and businesses."

Tony asked, "What do people think of solar energy? Do they like it?"

"Solar energy has many advantages. Energy from the sun is free, and we will never use it up. Solar energy is also quiet and clean. It does not smell or use water."

Sylvia raised her hand. "Are there any problems with solar energy?" she asked.

Mr. Thomas continued. "Some people do not like solar farms. They think the farms take up too much space or look ugly. Also, in most places, the sun usually does not shine all day. And, it never shines at night! For these reasons, they think solar energy is not worth the trouble. Some people want to use the land for something else."

"Thank you, Mr. Thomas," Pat's teacher said. "We learned a lot today!"

GO ON →

Name: _____ Date: _____

Use "The Solar Farm" to answer Numbers 6 through 10.

6 Read this sentence from the article.

> **See how the panels are installed, or placed,**
> **so they turn toward the sun?**

Which clue word from the sentence helps to explain
what *installed* means?

Ⓐ placed

Ⓑ turn

Ⓒ toward

7 Which evidence from the text explains how a solar
farm works?

Ⓐ Pat's class is studying energy resources.

Ⓑ "The panels turn the sun's energy into electricity."

Ⓒ "Solar energy is also quiet and clean."

8 Which of the following explains a benefit of solar energy?

Ⓐ Solar farms take up too much space.

Ⓑ Solar resources can produce renewable energy.

Ⓒ Solar panels are placed so they turn toward the sun.

GO ON →

9 What evidence from the text tells why some people do not like solar energy?

Ⓐ Solar farms take up too much space and are ugly.

Ⓑ Solar panels turn the sun's energy into electricity.

Ⓒ Solar farms do not smell or use water.

10 What is the MAIN idea of this article?

Ⓐ Solar energy may eventually get used up.

Ⓑ Solar farms are often built on old farm land.

Ⓒ Solar energy is a useful renewable resource.

STOP

9. What evidence from the text tells why some people do not like solar energy?

Ⓐ Solar farms take up too much space and energy.

Ⓑ Solar panels turn the sun's energy into electricity.

Ⓒ Solar farms do not smell or use water.

10. What is the MAIN idea of this article?

Ⓐ Solar energy may eventually get used up.

Ⓑ Solar farms are often built on old farm land.

Ⓒ Solar energy is a useful renewable resource.

Unit Assessment

Read "A Better Way" before you answer Numbers 1 through 7.

A Better Way

"Hey, Jess!" Calvin called out. "Do you want to go to a movie on Saturday? There is a new comedy playing in town."

"Sure," said Jess, "but I need a ride. Can your dad take us?"

"My dad is working. We can ride the bus, though," said Calvin.

"No way!" Jess answered loudly. "The bus takes forever to get into town. And it stops five blocks away from the movie theater."

Calvin frowned. "If only we had bikes," he thought. Then he **muttered** softly to himself, "But we don't."

That night, Calvin's dad helped him look for a cheap bike online. Calvin spotted a story on the Internet about a bike-sharing program in a nearby city. Calvin thought it sounded interesting. "How does bike sharing work?" he asked.

His dad explained, "It's easy. People sign up for the program. Then they can borrow a bike at any bike station in the city. They ride anywhere they want and return the bike to a station when they're done."

GO ON →

The Internet story was an **inspiration**. It made Calvin think. Maybe he could start a bike-sharing program in his own city. He asked his dad what he thought.

Calvin's dad nodded and then smiled. "I like that idea, and I bet other people will, too!"

Calvin and his dad made plans. They got together with friends and neighbors. They put their ideas together for a bike-sharing program. Then they presented their plan to the city council. The council liked the plan. They approved the program within months. The city had **funds**, or money, to buy new bikes. Soon, bike stations were appearing all over town.

That spring, Calvin asked Jess if she wanted to see a movie. "You can walk home with me after school," Calvin said. "But bring your bike helmet. We'll borrow bikes to get there!"

Use "A Better Way" to answer Numbers 1 through 7.

1 What is Calvin's MAIN problem in the passage?

Ⓐ His father does not have a car.

Ⓑ He cannot go to the movies with his friend.

Ⓒ He does not have a good way to get around town.

GO ON →

2 Read this paragraph from the passage.

> Calvin frowned. "If only we had bikes," he thought. Then he muttered softly to himself, "But we don't."

Which words in the paragraph give a clue about the meaning of *muttered*?

Ⓐ Calvin frowned

Ⓑ he thought

Ⓒ softly to himself

3 Read this sentence from the passage.

> The Internet story was an inspiration.

Which words from the text help you understand the meaning of *inspiration*?

Ⓐ It made Calvin think.

Ⓑ He asked his dad what he thought.

Ⓒ Calvin's dad nodded and then smiled.

4 What is the solution to Calvin's problem?

Ⓐ a new bike

Ⓑ a neighbor with a car

Ⓒ a bike-sharing program

GO ON →

5 What must happen BEFORE Calvin's solution can work?

Ⓐ The city council must like the plan.

Ⓑ Calvin's father must buy a bike.

Ⓒ Calvin must get a bike helmet.

6 Read this sentence from the passage.

The city had funds, or money, to buy new bikes.

Which word in the sentence means almost the SAME as *funds*?

Ⓐ city

Ⓑ money

Ⓒ bikes

7 What does Calvin do AFTER his problem is solved?

Ⓐ He builds bike stations with his friend.

Ⓑ He plans to borrow a city bike.

Ⓒ He rides his bike to school.

GO ON →

Read "Tsunami Warning!" before you answer Numbers 8 through 15.

Tsunami Warning!

A tsunami (soo-NAH-mee) is a big sea wave. It causes damage when it washes across the land. The effects can be **severe**, or very harsh. The waves can break buildings. They can sweep away trees and cars. A tsunami cannot be stopped. But scientists have a way to warn people when a tsunami is on the way.

A Movement in the Ocean

A tsunami is caused by a sudden movement in the ocean. The cause might be an earthquake. It might be a landslide. It might be some other powerful cause. The movement creates fast waves. As the waves get close to land, they do not **accelerate**. Instead, they slow down. They also become higher. When the waves hit the shore, they destroy things.

Tsunami Warning Systems

Years ago, people did not know when a tsunami was coming. Today, there are warning systems. These systems use sensors on the ocean floor. They measure changes in the ocean. Then, they send information about the changes to special devices. These devices float on top of the water.

GO ON →

From Satellite to Scientists

What happens next? The floating devices send the information to a satellite in space. Then, the satellite sends the information to a tsunami warning center. Scientists study the information. If a tsunami is on the way, they can let people know. Then, people can move to safety.

The warning systems can still be improved. They can be built in more places. An early warning is important. It is the only way to reduce the damage caused by tsunamis. Many lives may be saved by tsunami warning systems.

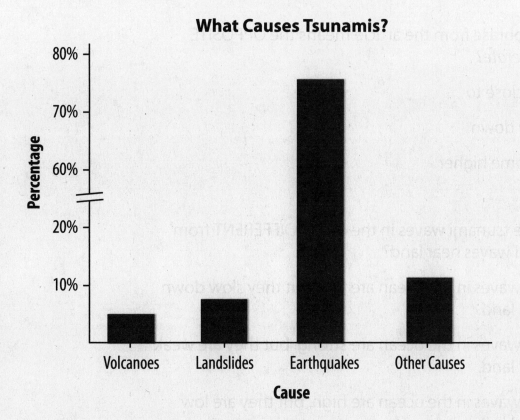

What Causes Tsunamis?

GO ON →

Use "Tsunami Warning!" to answer Numbers 8 through 15.

8 Read these sentences from the article.

> **The effects can be severe, or very harsh. The waves can break buildings.**

Which word from these sentences helps you understand the meaning of *severe*?

Ⓐ harsh

Ⓑ waves

Ⓒ buildings

9 Which phrase from the article means the OPPOSITE of *accelerate*?

Ⓐ get close to

Ⓑ slow down

Ⓒ become higher

10 How are tsunami waves in the ocean DIFFERENT from tsunami waves near land?

Ⓐ The waves in the ocean are fast, but they slow down near land.

Ⓑ The waves in the ocean are strong, but they are weak near land.

Ⓒ The waves in the ocean are high, but they are low near land.

GO ON →

11 What happens when a warning sensor feels changes in the ocean?

   Ⓐ The sensor sends information to a tsunami warning center.

   Ⓑ The sensor sends information to a satellite in space.

   Ⓒ The sensor sends information to a floating device.

12 What happens when scientists learn that a tsunami is on the way?

   Ⓐ They check that the satellites are working correctly.

   Ⓑ They send the information back to floating devices.

   Ⓒ They warn people so they can move to safety.

13 What is the MAIN idea of this article?

   Ⓐ It is important to have warning systems for tsunamis.

   Ⓑ Satellites send tsunami information around the world.

   Ⓒ Tsunamis are caused by sudden movements in the sea.

GO ON →

Tsunamis have more than one cause.

14 What detail from the article does the graph support?

   Ⓐ Tsunamis are a big problem.

   Ⓑ Tsunamis can have harmful effects.

   Ⓒ Tsunamis have more than one cause.

15 How do landslides and volcanoes compare as the cause of tsunamis?

   Ⓐ Volcanoes cause more tsunamis.

   Ⓑ Landslides cause more tsunamis.

   Ⓒ They cause the same number of tsunamis.

STOP

Read "The Endless Winter" before you answer Numbers 1 through 7.

The Endless Winter

Long ago, an endless winter settled onto the land. Clouds hid the sun. Snow and ice covered every bit of earth. The air was very cold, and the animals were frightened. There was no food or heat.

Five brave animals agreed to search for heat. They were Fox, Wolf, Caribou, Eagle, and Mink. They traveled a long way. Finally, they found a hidden doorway. They opened the door and saw a beautiful lake. Beside the lake was an igloo with two bear cubs inside. Three sacks hung on the wall of the igloo.

"Where is your mother?" Fox asked.

"She is fishing," the cubs said.

"And what is in the sacks?" Wolf asked.

"Our mother keeps rain in the first sack and wind in the second sack," the cubs said. "In the third sack, there is heat to keep us warm."

"Mother Bear is **selfish**," Wolf whispered. "She wants to keep all of the heat. She does not care about us. Surely she has some heat to share."

The friends left the igloo and made a plan. Caribou would go to the other side of the lake and distract Mother Bear. She would see him and paddle over to catch him. Then, Mink would chew a hole in the bear's canoe.

GO ON →

Their plan worked. Mother Bear was stranded on the other side of lake. The animals grabbed the sack of heat and hurried to the doorway. But the sack was large and hard to carry. So, the animals took turns carrying the sack as they **trudged** along with heavy steps. They inched closer and closer to the doorway. The animals grew weak and tired.

Soon, Mother Bear got back to shore. She began chasing the animals. Just as she was about to grab them, the sack fell on a sharp spear of ice and burst open. The heat rushed out, melting the ice and snow. Plants bloomed in the warm air. The animals danced and celebrated. This is why spring always follows winter in the order of the seasons.

Use "The Endless Winter" to answer Numbers 1 through 7.

1 Who is telling the story?

Ⓐ a speaker who is part of the story

Ⓑ a speaker who is not part the story

Ⓒ an animal who is described in the story

2 What must the friends do to help the animals in the passage?

Ⓐ They must find heat.

Ⓑ They must find food.

Ⓒ They must find a bear.

3 What does the narrator think of the five friends?

   Ⓐ They are selfish.

   Ⓑ They are brave.

   Ⓒ They are lucky.

4 Read this sentence from the passage.

   "Mother Bear is selfish," Wolf whispered.

What evidence from the text gives a clue about the meaning of *selfish*?

   Ⓐ Mother Bear keeps wind in the second sack.

   Ⓑ Mother Bear leaves her cubs to go fishing.

   Ⓒ Mother Bear wants to keep all of the heat.

5 Read this sentence from the passage.

   So, the animals took turns carrying the sack as they trudged along with heavy steps.

Which clue words tell the meaning of *trudged*?

   Ⓐ the animals took turns

   Ⓑ carrying the sack

   Ⓒ with heavy steps

GO ON →

Name: _____   Date: _____

6 What event do the details in the passage help to explain?

    Ⓐ why spring follows winter in the seasons

    Ⓑ why animals need heat to stay alive

    Ⓒ why plants bloom in warm air

7 What is an important lesson in this passage?

    Ⓐ Helping others takes a very long time.

    Ⓑ Working together helps a plan succeed.

    Ⓒ Fixing a problem is often dangerous work.

Copyright © McGraw-Hill Education. Permission is granted to reproduce for classroom use.

GO ON →

134   Grade 4

Unit Assessment · Unit 2

Read "Sea Partners" before you answer Numbers 8 through 15.

Sea Partners

An **ecosystem** is made up of different plants and animals. These living things all exist together in the same area. Many of the plants and animals depend on each other. Some of the animals work together as partners. One may protect the other. Or they may help each other find food.

Sea Anemones and Clownfish

The sea anemone (UH-nem-uh-nee) and the clownfish are partners. The anemone is beautiful. But it is dangerous. It has stinging tentacles. The sting is **poisonous**. It can be deadly, killing fish that swim too close. Then, the anemone eats the fish. But the clownfish is different. Its skin has a slimy coating. This protects it from the animal's sting. The clownfish feeds on what the anemone does not eat. It also cleans the anemone. In return, the anemone keeps the clownfish safe.

Imperial Shrimp and Sea Cucumbers

The Imperial shrimp and the sea cucumber are also partners. The Imperial shrimp rides on top of the sea cucumber. It hops off to find food. Then it hops back on when it is done. The sea cucumber does not seem to mind giving the shrimp a ride. No one knows if the shrimp actually helps the sea cucumber.

GO ON →

Remoras and Sharks

A remora is another type of fish. It does not swim well. But it cannot live without water flowing over its gills. The remora has a sucking disk on its body. It uses the disk to attach itself to a shark. As the shark swims, water rushes over the gills of the remora. The remora also helps the shark. It eats small parasites on the shark's body. This helps to keep the shark healthy. The shark hunts fish as its **prey**. But it does not eat the remora.

Shark and Remora Partnership

Parasites feed on the shark.

↓

The remora attaches to the shark.

↓

The remora eats parasites on the shark.

↓

The remora gets water through gills and food.

↓

The shark is free of parasites.

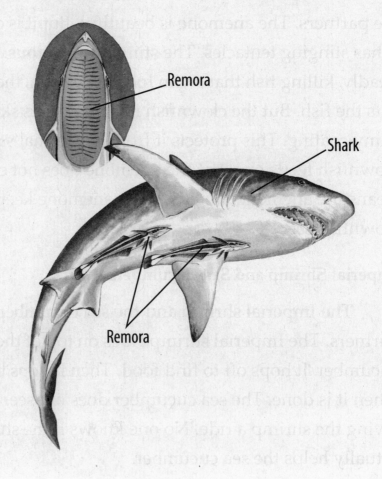

Remora

Shark

Remora

Use "Sea Partners" to answer Numbers 8 through 15.

8 Read this sentence from the article.

> **An ecosystem is made up of different plants and animals.**

Which sentence from the text tells the meaning of *ecosystem*?

Ⓐ These living things all exist together in the same area.

Ⓑ Many of the plants and animals depend on each other.

Ⓒ Some of the animals work together as partners.

9 Read these sentences from the article.

> **The sting is poisonous. It can be deadly, killing fish that swim too close.**

Which word from the sentences has about the SAME meaning as *poisonous*?

Ⓐ sting

Ⓑ deadly

Ⓒ close

10 Which key detail explains how the clownfish stays safe around sea anemones?

Ⓐ It hops off to find food.

Ⓑ It has stinging tentacles.

Ⓒ Its skin has a slimy coating.

GO ON →

11 Which sentence from the article BEST describes the relationship between the clownfish and the sea anemone?

Ⓐ The sea anemone and the clownfish are partners.

Ⓑ The clownfish feeds on what the anemone does not eat.

Ⓒ In return, the anemone keeps the clownfish safe.

12 Which sentence from the article describes how the sea cucumber helps the Imperial shrimp?

Ⓐ The Imperial shrimp and the sea cucumber are also partners.

Ⓑ The Imperial shrimp rides on top of the sea cucumber.

Ⓒ No one knows if the shrimp actually helps the sea cucumber.

13 Which sentence BEST describes how the remora and the shark work as partners?

Ⓐ The shark swims while the remora hunts prey.

Ⓑ The shark provides food and the remora cleans the shark.

Ⓒ The shark finds parasites and the remora wets the shark's gills.

GO ON →

14 Which word from the text is an example of a shark's *prey*?

Ⓐ fish

Ⓑ remora

Ⓒ parasites

15 Which BEST describes what the flow chart shows?

Ⓐ how the shark helps other animals

Ⓑ how the remora helps other animals

Ⓒ how the remora and shark help each other

STOP

Read "At Home in Space" before you answer Numbers 1 through 8.

At Home in Space

"Sara, it is time to pack your bags. I have a great new job," said Dad.

Sara started to **protest**. "Not again, Dad!" she complained. It was the fifth time her family had moved. Each time, Sara needed to learn her way around a new school. She hated to leave her friends on the basketball team, too.

Dad said, "This is a great chance. We are not just moving to a new colony this time. We are going to live on the space station! It will be a new adventure."

Sara did not want a new adventure. She wanted to stay where she was.

Three days later, Sara unpacked in her new home on the space station. She folded her clothes in a neat pile. But as soon as she turned her back, the clothes **scattered** in all directions toward the ceiling. Sara would have to get used to living without gravity. She would need to strap herself into bed or else she would float around while she slept.

A boy named Darren showed Sara around the school on her first day. Students from different planets talked cheerfully as they worked. A few of them smiled or held up two fingers as the galaxy's symbol of friendship.

GO ON →

Sara felt her shoulders start to relax as she visited the classes. The **tension** left her neck.

Giant melons and beans grew in tubes in the science room. Darren said, "We grow everything indoors. We keep lights on all the time. The air is always the perfect temperature. The plants love it here, just like the people!"

Sara grinned as she walked into the gym. The students were playing basketball. The players bounced high with each step. The lack of gravity changed the game, but it still looked like fun.

Sara was in the gym a few weeks later. The principal and a new student came in. Mr. Gray said, "Sara is one of our star players. She has become an important part of our school community in a short time."

Sara smiled at the new boy. She said, "Just ask if you need anything. You will love it here, too."

GO ON →

Name: _____ **Date:** _____

Use "At Home in Space" to answer Numbers 1 through 8.

1 Who is telling the story?

Ⓐ Sara

Ⓑ Sara's new principal

Ⓒ a narrator who is not part of the story

2 Read these sentences from the passage.

**Sara started to protest. "Not again, Dad!"
she complained.**

Which clue word helps to explain what *protest* means?

Ⓐ started

Ⓑ again

Ⓒ complained

3 What does Sara think about moving to space?

Ⓐ She does not want to leave her friends.

Ⓑ She does not want to make new friends.

Ⓒ She does not want to join the basketball team.

Copyright © McGraw-Hill Education. Permission is granted to reproduce for classroom use.

4 What does Sara's dad think about moving?

Ⓐ He is tired of changing jobs so often.

Ⓑ He is excited about a new adventure.

Ⓒ He is looking forward to making new friends.

5 Read this sentence from the passage.

But as soon as she turned her back, the clothes scattered in all directions toward the ceiling.

Which clue words help explain what *scattered* means?

Ⓐ turned her back

Ⓑ in all directions

Ⓒ toward the ceiling

6 Read this sentence from the passage.

The tension left her neck.

Which words from the text mean almost the OPPOSITE of *tension*?

Ⓐ while she slept

Ⓑ around the school

Ⓒ start to relax

GO ON →

7 How does Sara's point of view about her situation change?

Ⓐ She finds that she likes her new home and school.

Ⓑ She learns that she does not miss basketball after all.

Ⓒ She begins to forget about her friends in her old school.

8 With which statement would Sara MOST LIKELY agree?

Ⓐ Sometimes new experiences can bring good surprises and new friends.

Ⓑ While it is great to meet new people, they can never replace old friends.

Ⓒ It is always best to stay in a familiar place where you have friends.

Name: _____ **Date:** _____

Read "Gertrude Ederle, Channel Swimmer" before you answer Numbers 9 through 15.

Gertrude Ederle, Channel Swimmer

What happens to athletes when their careers end? Gertrude Ederle was one of the most famous swimmers ever. She found a way to help her community and keep doing the sport she loved.

Ederle's Early Years

Gertrude began to swim when she was very young. She had measles at age five. This disease hurt her hearing. "The doctors told me my hearing would get worse if I continued swimming, but I loved the water so much, I just couldn't stop," she said.

Gertrude began to compete in her teens. She held 29 swimming records between 1921 and 1925.

Swimming the English Channel

Gertrude wanted to swim across the English Channel. No woman had ever done this. It was 21 miles across. The idea made sense, and it seemed **logical** for Gertrude to try.

She did not succeed at first. After many hours, her team thought she was drowning. They wanted her to stop, but Gertrude **disagreed**. She told them they were wrong and she was just resting. Still, the judges made Gertrude stop.

Gertrude tried again, though. The next year, she covered her body with grease to stay warm. It was hard to swim straight in the cold, choppy water. Gertrude swam at least 35 miles before touching land!

Gertrude's success brought her fame. New York City held a parade in her honor. But the swim also made Gertrude's hearing get worse.

End of a Great Career

In 1933, Gertrude fell. The doctors said she might never walk again. Her career was over, too. But Gertrude proved the doctors wrong. Slowly, she got better. She also taught deaf children to swim. Gertrude chose to share the sport she loved with others.

Gertrude Ederle's Swimming Career

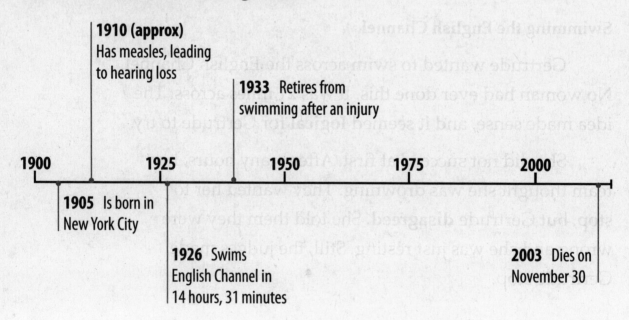

1910 (approx) Has measles, leading to hearing loss

1933 Retires from swimming after an injury

1900   1925   1950   1975   2000

1905 Is born in New York City

1926 Swims English Channel in 14 hours, 31 minutes

2003 Dies on November 30

GO ON →

Unit Assessment · Unit 3

Name: _____ **Date:** _____

Use "Gertrude Ederle, Channel Swimmer" to answer Numbers 9 through 15.

9 Why does the author include the quote by Gertrude in the second paragraph?

Ⓐ to show that Gertrude was a good swimmer

Ⓑ to show that Gertrude did not give up easily

Ⓒ to show that other people admired Gertrude

10 Read these sentences from the article.

> **No woman had ever done this. The idea made sense, and it seemed logical for Gertrude to try.**

Which words from the sentences have about the SAME meaning as *logical*?

Ⓐ done this

Ⓑ made sense

Ⓒ to try

11 Read this sentence from the article.

> **They wanted her to stop, but Gertrude disagreed.**

Which sentence in the article helps to explain what *disagreed* means?

Ⓐ Gertrude wanted to swim across the English Channel.

Ⓑ After many hours, her team thought she was drowning.

Ⓒ She told them they were wrong and she was just resting.

12 Which detail from the article supports the author's point of view that Gertrude was an inspiration to others?

Ⓐ Still, the judges made Gertrude stop.

Ⓑ New York City held a parade in her honor.

Ⓒ The doctors said she might never walk again.

13 Which statement BEST supports the author's opinion that Gertrude was involved in her community?

Ⓐ She taught swimming lessons to deaf children.

Ⓑ She proved the doctors wrong after her injury.

Ⓒ She was given a parade in New York City.

14 Which statement BEST states the author's point of view about Gertrude?

Ⓐ She was a very determined person.

Ⓑ She was a better swimmer than any man.

Ⓒ She changed people's ideas about education.

15 According to the time line, when did Gertrude swim across the English Channel?

Ⓐ 1910

Ⓑ 1926

Ⓒ 1933

STOP

Unit Assessment · Unit 3

Read "Andrew Jackson and the Stable Boy" before you answer Numbers 1 through 7.

Andrew Jackson and the Stable Boy

The tall man handed the reins of his horse to Peter. Without saying a word, he walked toward the White House.

"Peter, the President worked for a saddle maker when he was young," said Jacob, the stable manager.

Then the old man added, "You polish that saddle until it shines. One day, you might be polishing the President's boots! You know, President Jackson was captured by the British when he was your age. He refused to polish an officer's boots. He has been a British enemy ever since."

Peter whistled. No wonder Jackson had led the Americans to victory. The **overwhelming** win over the British in New Orleans had been an enormous success.

Peter went into the kitchen to fetch some apples for the President's horse. Mrs. Booker was there. She was making her special pancakes.

Suddenly, the tall man entered. Mrs. Booker was so surprised she dropped her spoon. Peter stood as still as he could. But inside he **squirmed** with excitement.

"Mrs. Booker, do I smell pancakes?" asked the President. "Have I told you about the ones my dear wife used to make? They're my favorite food in the world!"

"No, Sir," she replied.

GO ON →

The President picked up a pancake from the warm pan. He tipped a pitcher of molasses over it. Then, he popped it into his mouth. He left the kitchen humming.

Mrs. Booker smiled at Peter. She was pink with pride.

Peter returned to the stable. There, he listened to Jacob tell more stories about the President. He learned that Jackson grew up poor without a father. He had been a senator. Then he became a governor.

Jacob spoke passionately. "Never mind what people say. The President may not have come from a rich family. He may not have traveled the world. But he earned his way to office."

Peter could not believe his ears. The President grew up just like him? Old Jacob was right. You just had to earn your way in the world. Peter hurried back to the horses. He had work to do.

Use "Andrew Jackson and the Stable Boy" to answer Numbers 1 through 7.

1 Who is the narrator of this passage?

Ⓐ Peter, a stable boy

Ⓑ Mrs. Booker, the cook

Ⓒ a speaker outside the story

GO ON →

2 Read this paragraph from the passage.

> **Peter whistled. No wonder Jackson had led the Americans to victory. The overwhelming win over the British in New Orleans had been an enormous success.**

Which word from the paragraph has about the SAME meaning as *overwhelming*?

Ⓐ victory

Ⓑ enormous

Ⓒ success

3 Read this sentence from the passage.

> **But inside he squirmed with excitement.**

Which sentence from the passage helps to explain the meaning of *squirmed*?

Ⓐ Peter stood as still as he could.

Ⓑ Peter could not believe his ears.

Ⓒ Peter hurried back to the horses.

4 Which sentence BEST describes what Peter thinks of President Jackson?

Ⓐ He is afraid to work for the President.

Ⓑ He excited to meet the President.

Ⓒ He admires the President.

GO ON →

5 At the end of the passage, why does Peter plan to work hard at his job?

   Ⓐ He wants the President to make him manager of the stable.

   Ⓑ He sees how the President worked hard to get where he is.

   Ⓒ He knows that the President needs someone to shine his shoes.

6 Which sentence from the text BEST states the theme of the passage?

   Ⓐ No wonder Jackson had led the Americans to victory.

   Ⓑ The President may not have come from a rich family.

   Ⓒ You just had to earn your way in the world.

7 With which statement would Peter MOST LIKELY agree?

   Ⓐ There is more that divides people than unites them.

   Ⓑ All people have exactly the same experiences in life.

   Ⓒ People often have more in common than they realize.

GO ON →

Read "A Visit to the Planetarium" before you answer Numbers 8 through 15.

A Visit to the Planetarium

Our lucky fourth graders visited the planetarium this week. The trip was the final event of their space study.

The planetarium offers many different programs about space. Workers use telescopes to view the night sky. This **technology** helps them teach visitors about objects in our universe.

The Moon and Sun

The students studied different **phases** of the Moon. They learned how each stage in the Moon's cycle affects ocean tides. They saw how the Moon changes from a tiny **sliver** to a full circle each month. They also learned about eclipses of the Sun and Moon. They learned never to look directly at the Sun. They could hurt their eyes. The students also discovered how the Sun may change. Some day it may be cold and dark.

Constellations

The fourth graders got to visit the constellation exhibit, too. These groups of stars look like shapes in the sky. Ancient people gave the shapes names. They made up stories about them. Orion the Hunter is the students' favorite. That is because it is easy to spot in the night sky.

GO ON →

Space Exploration

Students even discovered what it is like to go to space. They watched a film about the first Moon landing. They also saw a model of the inside of a space shuttle.

The Space Show

The last part of the trip was the space show. Students went up to the observatory and found seats. They leaned back and settled in. The music began. The roof opened up. The lights got dim so students could see the night sky. It was a special night. They got to see meteors flash across the sky. That is something they will never forget.

Moon Phases

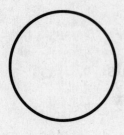  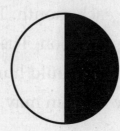 

| Full Moon | Waning Gibbous | Last Quarter | Waning Crescent |

GO ON →

Use "A Visit to the Planetarium" to answer Numbers 8 through 15.

8 Read this sentence from the article.

> **This technology helps them teach visitors about objects in our universe.**

Which evidence from the article gives an example of a type of *technology*?

Ⓐ Workers use telescopes to view the night sky.

Ⓑ These groups of stars look like shapes in the sky.

Ⓒ Students even discovered what it is like to go to space.

9 Read these sentences from the article.

> **The students studied different phases of the Moon. They learned how each stage in the Moon's cycle affects ocean tides.**

Which clue word from the sentences helps to explain what *phases* means?

Ⓐ stage

Ⓑ cycle

Ⓒ tides

GO ON →

10 According to the article, why should students avoid looking at the Sun?

Ⓐ It is too hard to see without a telescope.

Ⓑ It is only visible during an eclipse.

Ⓒ They could hurt their eyes.

11 Read this sentence from the article.

They saw how the Moon changes from a tiny sliver to a full circle each month.

Which words from the sentence mean almost the OPPOSITE of *sliver*?

Ⓐ the Moon changes

Ⓑ full circle

Ⓒ each month

12 Orion the Hunter is a favorite constellation because it _____.

Ⓐ is the largest object in space

Ⓑ has the most interesting story

Ⓒ is easy to find in the sky above

GO ON →

Name: _____ Date: _____

13 Which evidence from the text tells how the fourth graders learned what it is like to go to space?

Ⓐ They visited the constellation exhibit.

Ⓑ They saw a space show in the observatory.

Ⓒ They watched a film about the first Moon landing.

14 Which sentence in the article signals a cause-and-effect relationship?

Ⓐ Students went up to the observatory and found seats.

Ⓑ The lights got dim so students could see the night sky.

Ⓒ They got to see meteors flash across the sky.

15 According to the diagram, in which phase does the size of the Moon appear the smallest?

Ⓐ Waning Crescent

Ⓑ Waning Gibbous

Ⓒ Last Quarter

STOP

Read "Slue Foot Sue Rides Widow Maker" before you answer Numbers 1 through 7.

Slue Foot Sue Rides Widow Maker

You might have heard all about Pecos Bill. He was one of the boldest, most rugged cowboys in the West. Well, Pecos Bill decided it was time to find himself a wife. He wanted a girl who was as rough and tumble as he was. He didn't want some frilly, **fussy** thing.

Back then, ladies used to wear something called a hoop skirt under their long dresses. The bottom of the petticoat was round and bouncy. It was sort of like a hula hoop. One day, Pecos Bill saw a girl named Slue Foot Sue.

She was crossing a wide mud puddle. She did not wait for Pecos Bill to carry her across. She sat back. Then she bounced three times on the edge of her hoop skirt. She sailed right over the puddle. Then, she fixed her hat and walked on down the street.

Well, Pecos Bill thought that was **hilarious**. He laughed and laughed. Then, he asked Slue Foot Sue to marry him. That way he knew there would never be a dull moment with Sue around.

Sue said, "I'll marry you. But I have just one condition." Pecos Bill asked just what that would be. She said she wanted to ride his horse.

GO ON →

Now Pecos Bill's horse was rougher than its owner. Widow Maker was its name. The horse didn't like anyone riding it besides Bill. But Sue insisted. She wasn't going to marry Pecos Bill until he promised to share fair and square. So, finally he agreed.

Sue climbed onto that horse. She tucked her hoop skirt under her. Right away, Widow Maker started trying to throw her off. Sue fell off the horse. She didn't get hurt, though. She just bounced higher and higher until she bounced all the way up to the moon.

Sue was sad to be so far from home. She cried buckets of tears. Do you know how hard she cried? She filled the Mississippi River all the way from the land of the northern **territories** down to Louisiana. She cried so much her tears filled the sky all the way up to the moon.

Sue hopped off the moon and swam back home. She told Pecos Bill that next time, she thought she'd ride her own horse.

Name: _____ Date: _____

Use "Slue Foot Sue Rides Widow Maker" to answer Numbers 1 through 7.

1 Why does Pecos Bill choose Slue Foot Sue as a wife?

Ⓐ He wants a girl who is as rough and tumble as he is.

Ⓑ He wants a girl who can ride Widow Maker.

Ⓒ He wants a girl who wears a hoop skirt.

2 Which word from the passage means about the SAME as *fussy*?

Ⓐ boldest

Ⓑ rough

Ⓒ frilly

3 How does Slue Foot Sue solve the problem of crossing a wide mud puddle?

Ⓐ She waits for Pecos Bill to carry her across.

Ⓑ She uses her hat to walk across the puddle.

Ⓒ She bounces on the edge of her hoop skirt.

4 Why does Slue Foot Sue want to ride Bill's horse?

Ⓐ She wants Pecos Bill to ask her to marry him.

Ⓑ She wants Pecos Bill to share fair and square.

Ⓒ She wants to ride a horse with her hoop skirt.

5 Read this sentence from the passage.

Well, Pecos Bill thought that was hilarious.

Which sentence from the passage helps you understand
the meaning of *hilarious*?

Ⓐ She sailed right over the puddle.

Ⓑ He laughed and laughed.

Ⓒ Then, he asked Slue Foot Sue to marry him.

6 Which word from the passage has about the SAME
meaning as *territories*?

Ⓐ land

Ⓑ tears

Ⓒ time

7 How does Slue Foot Sue get back from the moon?

Ⓐ She rides Widow Maker home.

Ⓑ She bounces home.

Ⓒ She swims home.

GO ON →

Read "A Closer Look at Weaver Ants" before you answer Numbers 8 through 15.

A Closer Look at Weaver Ants

Ants are found in **tremendous**, or very large, numbers around the world. They have interesting habits. One of the most unusual kinds of ants is the weaver ant.

Tiny Tailors

Weaver ants have special talents. They weave leaves together to build their nests. Sometimes, weaver ants are called tailor ants. Like tailors, they use threads to make their nests.

It takes teamwork for weaver ants to make a nest. The first thing they need is a leaf. A single ant is too small to reach a leaf. So, the weaver ants send a message to other ants. They use a special chemical in their bodies. The other ants in the colony sense this chemical. Soon, more ants come to help. Next, the ants **cling** to each other. They grab on to form a living ant bridge. At last, other ants can cross the bridge to reach the leaves.

Next, they work together to bend the leaves. More ants come to help. They bring young ants. The young ants make silk. The grown ants squeeze drops of silk from the young ants. The drops form threads. Weaver ants use the thread to put the leaves together. Finally, these tiny ants have built a nest. It is the size of a soccer ball!

GO ON →

Ants Helping Trees

Imagine lots of these large ant nests up in the trees. It may look like the ants are hurting the trees. Instead, weaver ants help trees. They act like tiny guards. They keep birds away from the trees. They stop insects from eating the trees.

Ants Helping People

Did you know that weaver ants can help fight human sickness, too? They have a strong chemical inside them. The ants use this chemical to keep their nests safe. People use this chemical to make a medicine mixture. The medicine can fight infections.

Weaver ants are just one kind of ant. There are many others. They have interesting stories, too. All it takes is a curious mind and a close look to learn more about them.

Where Weaver Ants Live

KEY
■ Weaver Ant Habitats

GO ON →

Use "A Closer Look at Weaver Ants" to answer Numbers 8 through 15.

8   Read these sentences from the article.

> **Ants are found in tremendous, or very large, numbers around the world. They have interesting habits.**

Which word or words from the sentences mean about the SAME as *tremendous*?

Ⓐ very large

Ⓑ around the world

Ⓒ interesting

9   How do weaver ants solve the problem of making nests?

Ⓐ They use medicine mixtures.

Ⓑ They use leaves they fit together.

Ⓒ They use pieces of clothing they find.

10   What is the FIRST thing a weaver ant does when it cannot reach a leaf?

Ⓐ It sends a message to other ants.

Ⓑ It carries young ants to the leaf.

Ⓒ It crosses an ant bridge.

GO ON →

11 Read these sentences from the article.

> **Soon, more ants come to help. Next, the ants cling to each other. They grab on to form a living ant bridge.**

Which phrase from the sentences has about the SAME meaning as *cling*?

Ⓐ come to help

Ⓑ grab on

Ⓒ living ant bridge

12 What is the LAST step weaver ants must do to get to the leaves they need?

Ⓐ They must guard the tree they find.

Ⓑ They must create a type of medicine.

Ⓒ They must cross a bridge of living ants.

13 Which evidence from the text tells what the ants do once they have the leaves?

Ⓐ At last, other ants can cross the bridge to reach the leaves.

Ⓑ Next, they work together to bend the leaves.

Ⓒ They keep birds away from the trees.

GO ON →

14 How do weaver ants keep the leaves together in their new nest?

Ⓐ They cut the leaves.

Ⓑ They build a bridge.

Ⓒ They use threads of silk.

15 According to the map, in which continent can weaver ants be found?

Ⓐ South America

Ⓑ North America

Ⓒ Africa

STOP

Read "Alita's Family Tree" before you answer Numbers 1 through 7.

Alita's Family Tree

It was a sunny spring morning in the year 1970. Alita sat on her grandmother's porch as a sprinkler sprayed a fine **mist** of water over a flower garden. The two were waiting for a cake to finish baking.

"Abuela, I can't believe Great-Uncle Rico is coming to live in Arizona for good!" said Alita.

"Sí," said Abuela. "My brother is leaving Mexico. He is coming to live in the United States."

"How old were you when you came to the United States?" Alita asked.

"I came here when I was a teenager. I was the **eldest** child in the family," Abuela replied. "All my brothers and sisters were younger than me."

Soon, the cake was ready. Uncle Paco pulled up in his truck. Alita's father came out to the porch to help his brother. They started setting up for the welcoming party.

The men pushed Abuela's big oak table over to the side of the porch. Paco paused for a moment. "I remember that old farm table we used to play with when we were kids."

Alita's father nodded. "Yes, it's funny what we remember about the past."

GO ON →

Alita thought about her growing and changing family. She said, "I wish there was a way to organize information about family members."

"Why not start a family tree?" Uncle Paco suggested. "You can put Dad and me on the tree. Then you can add your grandparents on each side of the family. You can go back even further if you want."

Abuela showed her a family tree chart in an old book.

By then, the cake had cooled, so Alita used frosting to make a tree on the top. It was meant to stand for the family. Alita took Abuela's book home with her that evening and copied the tree chart onto a piece of paper. Then, she began to fill it in.

Years later, Alita grew up, got married, and had a daughter of her own. One day, she came across the old family tree she had made.

Alita showed the family tree to her daughter and explained how people on the tree were connected. Margie loved the stories. She wanted to add to the family tree.

"I can use my computer to keep adding to the tree," said Margie.

Alita smiled. She hoped Margie would use the family tree to tell her own children about the past.

GO ON →

Use "Alita's Family Tree" to answer Numbers 1 through 7.

1 Which words from the passage give a clue about the meaning of *mist*?

(A) spring morning

(B) sprinkler sprayed

(C) a flower garden

2 What does Alita learn from Abuela?

(A) why Great-Uncle Rico is coming to live in Arizona

(B) what Abuela's life was like growing up in Mexico

(C) when Abuela came to the United States

3 Which clue words in the passage help to explain what *eldest* means?

(A) coming to live

(B) when I was a teenager

(C) younger than me

4 What does Alita learn about from Uncle Paco?

(A) her father's childhood

(B) Abuela's big oak table

(C) the welcoming party

Name: _____   **Date:** _____

5 How does Alita organize information about her family members?

Ⓐ She bakes a special cake.

Ⓑ She creates a tree chart.

Ⓒ She talks to her father.

6 Who will likely continue adding to the history of Alita's family?

Ⓐ Alita's daughter Margie

Ⓑ Alita's great-uncle

Ⓒ Alita's Abuela

7 What is the overall message of this passage?

Ⓐ It is fun to listen to family stories.

Ⓑ It is important to keep a record of the past.

Ⓒ It is better to think about the future than the past.

Read "A Simple Savings Plan" before you answer Numbers 8 through 15.

A Simple Savings Plan

Every week, I get an allowance. I also make money working around the neighborhood. But I usually **consume** my earnings, using up cash quickly. Many students have this problem. So what can we do? I talked to my parents about money matters. They shared some good tips. This is what I learned.

Banking Facts

You do not have to be an **entrepreneur** who starts a business to make money. You can make money just by putting cash into a bank. Banking has been around for thousands of years. Ancient Greece and Rome had banking systems. In the United States today, the government watches over the way banking is done. As a result, banks are safe places for our money.

Opening a Savings Account

What kind of bank account should we open? It seems like the best account for students is a savings account. Many banks do not charge fees for having a savings account. And they pay interest on the money we put in.

But what if the interest rate is low? What if we earn only pennies a month? A bank is still a good place to keep money. Having an account may even make us want to save more. It is fun to watch your money grow!

GO ON →

Fun and the Future

Saving money does not mean that we have to **forfeit**, or give up, having fun. We can put half our money into a savings account. Then we can use the other half for things we enjoy. If we're smart, we can save lots of money for the future. And we still have fun spending a little today!

Glossary

account (UH•KOUNT) an arrangement you have with a bank to keep money there

fees (FEEZ) money that a bank charges you for services

interest (IN•TRIST) money paid to you for keeping your savings at a bank

GO ON →

Use "A Simple Savings Plan" to answer Numbers 8 through 15.

8 Read this sentence from the article.

> **But I usually consume my earnings, using up cash quickly.**

Which word or words from the sentence have about the SAME meaning as *consume*?

Ⓐ usually

Ⓑ using up

Ⓒ quickly

9 What evidence from the text gives a clue about the meaning of *entrepreneur*?

Ⓐ starts a business

Ⓑ make money

Ⓒ watches over

10 Which sentence from the article tells why a bank is a safe place for your money?

Ⓐ You can make money just by putting cash into a bank.

Ⓑ Banking has been around for thousands of years.

Ⓒ In the United States today, the government watches over the way banking is done.

GO ON →

11 What happens to your money when you have a savings account at a bank?

Ⓐ You get interest on the money in the account.

Ⓑ You pay the bank interest for the money in the account.

Ⓒ You must keep your money in the account for many years.

12 Read this sentence from the article.

Saving money does not mean that we have to forfeit, or give up, having fun.

Which words from the sentence have about the SAME meaning as *forfeit*?

Ⓐ saving money

Ⓑ give up

Ⓒ having fun

13 According to the article, how can you have fun while also saving money?

Ⓐ Put all your money in a savings account.

Ⓑ Put a little money in savings and spend the rest.

Ⓒ Put half your money in savings and spend the other half.

GO ON →

14 What is the MAIN idea of this article?

    Ⓐ Banks have been around for a long time.

    Ⓑ It is good to have fun and spend your money.

    Ⓒ Having a bank savings account is a good idea.

15 According to the glossary at the end of the article, what does the word *fees* mean in the text?

    Ⓐ money that a bank charges for services

    Ⓑ an arrangement to keep money in a bank

    Ⓒ money paid for keeping savings at a bank

STOP

Exit
Assessment

Read "The Secret" before you answer Numbers 1 through 7.

The Secret

Laura looked around the lunchroom for her friends, Miki and Alma. The girls always ate lunch together, but today her friends were not there. Laura thought it was strange as she sat down at a table by herself.

After school, she saw Miki and Alma whispering together. When they saw her, they turned and walked to their buses. Laura was confused. What did she do wrong?

When she got home, Laura told her mother about the problem. "I think Miki and Alma have a secret," she said, "and they don't want me to know about it. I felt **humiliated** when they whispered together and then walked away without including me."

"You shouldn't feel foolish," Mom said in a caring voice. "Miki and Alma are probably just working on a special project together."

Laura sighed and picked up her books. She walked upstairs to do her homework. "Maybe things will be different tomorrow," she thought to herself.

About an hour later, the doorbell rang. Then Laura heard the hushed whispers of her friends' voices in the hallway. She crept to the top of the stairs and looked down.

"Dad took us to pick him up," Miki was saying.

GO ON →

"Your father is so **gracious** to help," Laura's mother said. "And you girls have been so kind and helpful!"

Then Laura noticed a crate by her mother's feet. She walked downstairs. "What's going on?" she said, looking from her mother to her friends.

"Well, you've wanted a dog for a long time," Mom said smiling. "So last month, I made an **inquiry** into adopting a puppy. My search for information led me to a dog rescue group. I asked Miki and Alma to help pick out a puppy for you!"

"He needed shots and a checkup before he could go home," Miki said. "We just picked him up from the vet."

Miki opened the dog crate and a bundle of fur tumbled out. Laura knelt down and opened her arms. The puppy ran to her and licked her face.

"Oh, he's perfect!" Laura cried. Then she looked up at her friends. "Thanks! This is the best secret in the world!"

Use "The Secret" to answer Numbers 1 though 7.

1 What problem does Laura have in the passage?

   Ⓐ She does not have any friends.

   Ⓑ Her friends do not want to talk to her.

   Ⓒ Her friends tell her secrets to other people.

2 What do Miki and Alma do RIGHT AFTER Laura sees them whispering?

   Ⓐ They walk to their buses.

   Ⓑ They eat lunch with Laura.

   Ⓒ They talk to Laura's mother.

3 Read this sentence from the passage.

   "I felt humiliated when they whispered together and then walked away without including me."

   Which word from the passage has about the SAME meaning as *humiliated*?

   Ⓐ confused

   Ⓑ foolish

   Ⓒ caring

4 Which word from the passage helps you understand the meaning of *gracious*?

Ⓐ father

Ⓑ kind

Ⓒ crate

5 How is Laura's problem solved?

Ⓐ She learns that her friends are playing a game.

Ⓑ She learns that her friends do not have a secret.

Ⓒ She learns that her friends are helping her mother.

6 Which words from the passage give a clue about the meaning of *inquiry*?

Ⓐ search for information

Ⓑ led me to

Ⓒ help pick out

7 What helpful thing do Miki and Alma do at the END of the passage?

Ⓐ They pick up the puppy from the vet.

Ⓑ They choose a puppy to give to Laura.

Ⓒ They do not tell Laura about the puppy.

Read "America's Favorite Skyscraper" before you answer
Numbers 8 through 15.

America's Favorite Skyscraper

Visitors love the sights of New York City. The Empire
State Building is one of the most popular of all. Millions of
visitors come to see the building each year. But it is much
more than just a tall building. It is one of the greatest
skyscrapers ever built!

Breaking the World Record

If you lived in New York between 1928 and 1930,
you would have watched the Chrysler Building being
built. When it was finished, it was the tallest building in
the world. But soon, another skyscraper topped it. That
was the Empire State Building. The Empire State Building
was finished in 1931. It became the tallest building of all.
It no longer holds the record today, but it is still famous.

Building a Great Skyscraper

The project of building the Empire State Building
was an enormous **undertaking**. Tons of materials and
thousands of workers were needed for the project. The
task was huge, yet it was completed in only about a year.

The Empire State Building was built to last. It is
made of steel and other materials. It has **substantial**, or
great, strength. The building can resist lightning strikes.
It is so strong that when a plane hit it in 1945, it was not
badly damaged.

GO ON →

A View from the Top

The Empire State Building was built for visitors. It has two viewing decks. From these decks, people have a wide view of the city. The view is one of the best in New York. It keeps visitors coming back year after year.

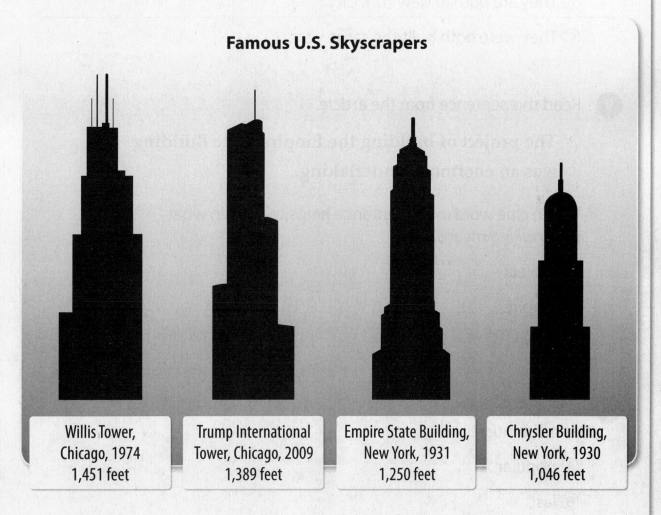

Famous U.S. Skyscrapers

Willis Tower,
Chicago, 1974
1,451 feet

Trump International
Tower, Chicago, 2009
1,389 feet

Empire State Building,
New York, 1931
1,250 feet

Chrysler Building,
New York, 1930
1,046 feet

GO ON ➤

Name: _____ Date: _____

Use "America's Favorite Skyscraper" to answer Numbers 8 through 15.

8 How are the Empire State Building and Chrysler Building ALIKE?

Ⓐ They are both the same height.

Ⓑ They are both in New York City.

Ⓒ They were both built the same year.

9 Read this sentence from the article.

> **The project of building the Empire State Building was an enormous undertaking.**

Which clue word in the sentence helps to explain what *undertaking* means?

Ⓐ project

Ⓑ empire

Ⓒ state

10 Which word from the article has about the SAME meaning as *substantial*?

Ⓐ popular

Ⓑ last

Ⓒ great

11 Why wasn't the Empire State Building badly damaged when a plane hit it in 1945?

Ⓐ The plane was small.

Ⓑ The building is very strong.

Ⓒ The building was still being built.

12 Why do visitors keep coming back to the Empire State Building?

Ⓐ There are good views from the viewing decks.

Ⓑ It is more famous than the Chrysler Building.

Ⓒ It is in the middle of New York City.

13 What is the MAIN idea of this article?

Ⓐ New York City has wonderful things to see and do.

Ⓑ Many of the tallest buildings in the world are in the United States.

Ⓒ The Empire State Building is one of the greatest skyscrapers ever built.

GO ON →

14 Which famous U.S. skyscraper in the graph is the tallest?

Ⓐ Willis Tower

Ⓑ Empire State Building

Ⓒ Trump International Tower

15 Which detail from the article does the graph support?

Ⓐ The Empire State Building is not the tallest skyscraper any longer.

Ⓑ The Empire State Building is an unusual skyscraper.

Ⓒ The Empire State Building is the oldest skyscraper.

STOP

Read "The Hare and the Lion" before you answer Numbers 1 through 7.

The Hare and the Lion

A Tale from East Africa

The lion and the hare were enemies. The lion had tried to catch the hare many times, but the tricky rabbit always fooled him.

One day, the lion asked everyone he met, "Where does the hare live?"

All the people said, "We do not know, for the hare and his wife have left. They did not tell us where they were going."

The lion searched for many days. At last, he found someone who knew where the hare lived. "That is his house," the man said as he pointed to the top of a high hill.

The lion climbed the steep path until he found the house and pounded on the door. "Come out, hare," the lion demanded, but the house was silent. No one was home.

"It is time I fooled that hare. I will hide in the house," the lion said. "When the hare comes home with his wife, I will catch them both."

The hare and his wife soon returned. As they started to climb the path, the hare saw the tracks that the lion's paws had made. "Please, go back," the hare **requested**, asking his wife in a polite voice. "The lion has come this way and is looking for me."

GO ON →

When his wife left, the hare continued on, following the tracks that led into his house. "The lion must be inside," he thought.

The hare stood far from the house and called out, "Hello, house!"

When there was no reply, the hare asked, "What is wrong, house? You always reply when I greet you. Today there must be someone inside."

Without thinking, the lion answered, "Hello!"

"Oh, lion!" the hare called. "You are inside. It seems that I have fooled you again. Don't you know that a house does not talk?"

"Wait right there," the lion growled angrily, but the hare did not wait. Instead, he ran away as fast as he could.

The lion chased the hare until he was very tired, but he could not catch the rabbit. **Frustrated**, he said, "I am too discouraged to go any further. The hare has fooled me for the last time."

And so the poor lion turned around and went home.

GO ON →

Use "The Hare and the Lion" to answer Numbers 1 through 7.

1 What does the hare do to the lion again and again?

Ⓐ fool him

Ⓑ catch him

Ⓒ search for him

2 Who is telling this story?

Ⓐ the lion in the passage

Ⓑ the hare in the passage

Ⓒ a narrator not in the passage

3 What does the speaker think about the hare?

Ⓐ He is tricky.

Ⓑ He is foolish.

Ⓒ He is honest.

4 Read these sentences from the passage.

"Please go back," the hare requested, asking his wife in a polite voice. "The lion has come this way and is looking for me."

What evidence from the sentences gives a clue about the meaning of *requested*?

Ⓐ asking his wife

Ⓑ has come this way

Ⓒ is looking for me

GO ON →

5 Read this paragraph from the passage.

> The lion chased the hare until he was very tired, but he could not catch the rabbit. Frustrated, he said, "I am too discouraged to go any further. The hare has fooled me for the last time."

Which word from the paragraph has about the SAME meaning as *frustrated*?

Ⓐ tired

Ⓑ discouraged

Ⓒ fooled

6 Which sentence from the passage shows what the speaker thinks about the lion?

Ⓐ The lion searched for many days.

Ⓑ Without thinking, the lion answered, "Hello!"

Ⓒ And so the poor lion turned around and went home.

7 What important lesson does this passage teach?

Ⓐ Always run away from trouble when you can.

Ⓑ Be honest and you will not likely be fooled by others.

Ⓒ Sometimes it is better to walk away after trying your best.

GO ON →

Exit Assessment · Unit 2

Read "Living on the Edge: Tide Pool Creatures" before you answer Numbers 8 through 15.

Living on the Edge: Tide Pool Creatures

When the ocean tide is low, pools of saltwater collect near rocky shores. The animals living in these pools face many challenges. They get dry from the hot sun. Predators can attack them. They get swept back and forth by high winds. The rising tide brings waves of freezing water. Yet, they can hang on. These creatures are **fragile** and can be easily hurt. It is hard to survive. Here are some amazing tide pool creatures.

Mussels

Mussels are a type of mollusk. They look like tiny clams. They have two hard shells that protect the body inside. Mussels survive by attaching to rocks. At high tide, they open their shells just a crack. The seawater then washes in bits of food.

Sea Stars

Sea stars eat mussels. When a sea star attacks a mussel, its body becomes stiff. It uses its sucker feet to grab onto the mussel. Then it pulls open the shell. The sea star uses an unusual method for eating that is **extraordinary**. It pushes its stomach out of its body and into the shell. When it is done, it pulls its stomach back into its body.

GO ON →

The sea star also hunts limpets. A limpet is another animal with a shell. Unlike mussels, a limpet can move around. It has a strong muscle that it **ripples**, or moves back and forth, in waves. This muscle is like a foot to move around on. It can help the limpet escape from the sea star.

Sea Urchins

Sea urchins also have shells for protection. Their shells are covered with many spines that can sting. They move on tiny tube feet to find plants to eat. In tide pools, sea urchins may dig into the rocks. This protects them from strong waves. It also helps keep them hidden from predators who want to eat them.

Ocean Tides and Limpets

The tide goes out and the water level lowers.	→	Limpets grip the rocks, trapping water under their shells to survive.	→	The tide comes in and the water level rises.	→	Limpets begin to move around, searching for food.

GO ON →

Use "Living on the Edge: Tide Pool Creatures" to answer Numbers 8 through 15.

8 What is the MAIN idea of the first paragraph of the article?

Ⓐ Tide pool animals face challenges to survive.

Ⓑ Tide pool animals get dry from the hot sun.

Ⓒ Tide pool animals are amazing creatures.

9 Read these sentences from the article.

> **The rising tide brings waves of freezing water. Yet, they can hang on. These creatures are fragile and can be easily hurt. It is hard to survive.**

Which words from the article have a similar meaning to the word *fragile*?

Ⓐ rising tide

Ⓑ easily hurt

Ⓒ hard to survive

10 Which sentence from the article tells how mussels get food?

Ⓐ They have two hard shells that protect the body inside.

Ⓑ Mussels survive by attaching to rocks.

Ⓒ At high tide, they open their shells just a crack.

11 Which detail from the article tells how a sea star eats a mussel?

Ⓐ When a sea star attacks a mussel, its body becomes stiff.

Ⓑ It uses its sucker feet to grab onto the mussel.

Ⓒ It pushes its stomach out of its body and into the shell.

12 Read this sentence from the article.

> The sea star uses an unusual method for eating that is extraordinary.

Which clue word from the sentence helps to explain what *extraordinary* means?

Ⓐ unusual

Ⓑ method

Ⓒ eating

13 Read these sentences from the article.

> It has a strong muscle that it ripples, or moves back and forth, in waves. This muscle is like a foot to move around on.

What evidence from the sentences tells the meaning of *ripples*?

Ⓐ has a strong muscle

Ⓑ moves back and forth

Ⓒ is like a foot

14 Which detail tells how sea urchins stay protected from strong waves?

Ⓐ They have shells covered with spines.

Ⓑ They move on tiny tube feet.

Ⓒ They may dig into the rocks.

15 In the flow chart, what do limpets do when the tide comes in?

Ⓐ They grip the rocks.

Ⓑ They move to look for food.

Ⓒ They trap water under their shells.

STOP

Read "The Liberty Guide" before you answer Numbers 1 through 8.

The Liberty Guide

"I can't wait to see Philadelphia!" said James to his brother Amos. "In school, I learned that this city is an important part of history."

James's family had come to Philadelphia to visit Amos, who was in his first year of college there.

The brothers went into a bookstore and Amos picked up a guidebook. He said, "This one looks **trustworthy**. We can depend on it to show us where to go in the city."

Amos opened the book and asked his brother, "Where should we go first?"

"I suggest that you start at Declaration House," said a loud voice.

The boys jumped back as Amos said, "Wow! I think we just bought a talking book!"

The book repeated, "First stop, Declaration House. This is where Thomas Jefferson wrote the Declaration of Independence. This document is an important **proclamation** that tells why the colonies wanted to be free from England. It also lists the **injustices** of the king. It tells about the unfair things he did."

GO ON →

"Constitution Hall is next," continued the book. "The Founding Fathers approved the Declaration here. These men worked to free the colonies. They signed the Constitution here, too. It lists the rights of citizens and tells what kind of government we have."

The boys visited both places in the city before stopping at Congress Hall.

The voice said, "This is where Congress met when John Adams became President. Adams was one of the Founding Fathers. He believed that liberty is every person's right. You enjoy liberty today because of the great work of men like Adams."

The last stop was the Liberty Bell. James asked the book, "Will we hear it ring?"

"No, the bell cracked the first time it rang. It still stands as a symbol of our freedom, though," explained the book.

"Wow!" said James. "I didn't realize that history could be so interesting."

The two brothers couldn't wait to see what the book would describe next.

Name: _____ Date: _____

Use "The Liberty Guide" to answer Numbers 1 through 8.

1 Who is the narrator of the passage?

Ⓐ James

Ⓑ a talking book

Ⓒ a speaker not in the story

2 What does James think about visiting Philadelphia?

Ⓐ He would rather talk to the book than visit the city.

Ⓑ He is excited to see the city because he learned about it in school.

Ⓒ He wants Amos to show him around the city so that he can go to college there, too.

3 Read these sentences from the passage.

> "This one looks trustworthy. We can depend on it to show us where to go in the city."

Which phrase from the sentences helps to explain what *trustworthy* means?

Ⓐ depend on it

Ⓑ to show us

Ⓒ where to go

GO ON →

198 Grade 4

Exit Assessment · Unit 3

Copyright © McGraw-Hill Education. Permission is granted to reproduce for classroom use.

4 What does Amos think when the brothers discover the talking book?

Ⓐ He is frightened.

Ⓑ He is confused.

Ⓒ He is surprised.

5 Read this sentence from the passage.

"This document is an important proclamation that tells why the colonies wanted to be free from England."

Which word from the sentence helps to explain the meaning of *proclamation*?

Ⓐ document

Ⓑ colonies

Ⓒ England

6 Read these sentences from the passage.

"It also lists the injustices of the king. It tells about the unfair things he did."

Which word from these sentences gives a clue about the meaning of *injustices*?

Ⓐ lists

Ⓑ king

Ⓒ unfair

GO ON →

7 What do James and Amos think about the Liberty Bell?

Ⓐ It is a symbol for liberty.

Ⓑ It does not belong in Philadelphia.

Ⓒ It is the most important site in the city.

8 With which statement would James and Amos MOST LIKELY agree?

Ⓐ The best city in the United States is Philadelphia.

Ⓑ Philadelphia should be called the Cradle of Liberty.

Ⓒ The bookstore is an important part of the city of Philadelphia's history.

GO ON →

Read "Harriet Beecher Stowe, a Woman of Words" before you answer Numbers 9 through 15.

Harriet Beecher Stowe, a Woman of Words

The dinner table was a noisy place at the Beecher home. Harriet Beecher's father taught his 11 children how to state their opinions clearly. Many great discussions happened at that dinner table.

Born to Write

The Beecher children were also taught to make a difference in the world. Harriet won an essay contest before she was ten. Her father was very proud. Harriet said it was the best day of her life. She decided she would make a difference by writing.

Words for Change

Harriet moved to Ohio and married Calvin Stowe. They had seven children. Over time, Harriet met former slaves and listened to their stories.

When Harriet's young son died, she was deeply saddened. She remembered the stories of the slaves. Now she understood how they felt when their children were taken away.

A publisher asked Harriet to "paint a word picture of slavery." She wrote stories that he printed in his newspaper.

GO ON →

Uncle Tom's Cabin

Harriett wrote story after story. Readers begged for more. The stories were published in a book called *Uncle Tom's Cabin*. The book sold 1.5 million copies in one year. Harriet's words began to change the way people thought about slavery.

Back then, large farms could not run without slaves. Their work was important to the business of **agriculture**, or farming. Many people did not want to end slavery for this reason. When the Civil War began, the country was divided over whether slavery was right or wrong.

In 1862, Harriett met President Abraham Lincoln. Some say he told Harriet, "So you're the little woman who wrote the book that started this great war."

Harriet Speaks Out

Many groups tried to end slavery. These **organizations** sent letters asking for Harriet's help. She traveled to Europe where she attended meetings and spoke out against slavery.

Harriet wrote many books in her lifetime, but the words of *Uncle Tom's Cabin* brought the greatest change to the U.S.

The Life of Harriet Beecher Stowe

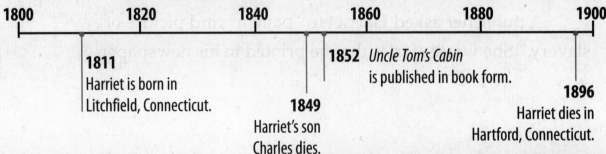

| 1800 | 1820 | 1840 | 1860 | 1880 | 1900 |

1811
Harriet is born in Litchfield, Connecticut.

1849
Harriet's son Charles dies.

1852 *Uncle Tom's Cabin* is published in book form.

1896
Harriet dies in Hartford, Connecticut.

GO ON →

Name: _____ **Date:** _____

Use "Harriet Beecher Stowe, a Woman of Words" to answer Numbers 9 through 15.

9 Based on the article, which event would the author MOST LIKELY think had the greatest influence in Harriet's life?

Ⓐ Harriet made her father proud by winning an essay contest when she was a child.

Ⓑ Harriet married Calvin Stowe and had many children with him.

Ⓒ Harriet met President Lincoln during the time of the Civil War.

10 Which word from the article has almost the SAME meaning as *agriculture*?

Ⓐ business

Ⓑ farming

Ⓒ slavery

11 Which point of view does the quotation from President Abraham Lincoln support?

Ⓐ Harriet had the power to end slavery.

Ⓑ Harriet knew many different famous people.

Ⓒ Harriet's stories led to important events and changes.

GO ON →

Exit Assessment · Unit 3   Grade 4   **203**

12 Which word from the article has almost the SAME meaning as *organizations*?

Ⓐ groups

Ⓑ letters

Ⓒ meetings

13 What evidence from the text BEST supports the author's point of view that people respected Harriet?

Ⓐ She married Calvin Stowe and had seven children.

Ⓑ She had the opportunity to meet President Lincoln.

Ⓒ She was asked to go to Europe to speak against slavery.

14 With which of the following statements would the author MOST LIKELY agree?

Ⓐ People who succeed as children will also succeed as adults.

Ⓑ People who state their opinions will be remembered in history.

Ⓒ People can bring about change by writing about what they believe in.

15 Which statement does the time line BEST support?

Ⓐ Harriet decided she would make a difference by writing.

Ⓑ Harriet wrote *Uncle Tom's Cabin* soon after her son died.

Ⓒ Harriet wrote many other books after *Uncle Tom's Cabin*.

STOP

Read "Life in a Soddy" before you answer Numbers 1 through 7.

Life in a Soddy

"Louisa, hand me that broom," said Mama. She stood on a wooden chair and reached up to knock down a snake **dangling** from the ceiling. It swung loosely from a roof pole. Then, she swept it out the door of the sod house.

Louisa noticed how **weary** her mother looked. No wonder she always seemed tired. She cooked and cleaned from morning till night. She spent hours heating water in a big pot on the stove. Her mother only seemed to rest for the Fourth of July picnic each summer.

"Louisa, put the baby in the cradle."

Louisa did as she was told and then rocked the cradle with her foot. She started to sew up the hole in a sock. "Mama, will we ever live in a real house?" she asked.

Her mother bit her lip. She said, "This is a real house. It is warm in winter and cool in summer."

Louisa said, "But Mama, every time it rains, muddy water drips through the dirt roof, and my dress is always dusty from touching the dirt floor."

"Why, it is so much brighter than when we lived underground in the old dugout. At least now we have two windows," said Mama.

GO ON →

Louisa had to agree. This mud brick house was better than the dugout. Her family had built the old dugout when they first moved to Nebraska. After a few years, they had cut bricks of prairie grass to build the new sod house. Now, Louisa rarely went into the old dugout except to feed the chickens in winter.

"All things in good time," said Mama. "It is 1879, and many families today would be happy as kings to live in a nice, warm house like this. We should be thankful for what we have now."

Louisa picked up a piece of chalk. She drew a picture on the slate chalkboard she used for school. It showed a house with a wooden roof and many windows. She imagined what the new type of house would look like inside. Her **version** would have more than one room. It would have a dry ceiling and a wooden floor. It would be clean and bright.

Louisa made herself a promise. One day, she would have a home like the one she drew. She hoped her mama could come live in it with her.

GO ON →

Use "Life in a Soddy" to answer Numbers 1 through 7.

1 Who is the narrator of this passage?

Ⓐ Louisa

Ⓑ Louisa's mother

Ⓒ a speaker outside the story

2 Read these sentences from the passage.

> **She stood on a wooden chair and reached up to knock down a snake dangling from the ceiling. It swung loosely from a roof pole.**

Which phrase from the sentences gives a clue about the meaning of *dangling*?

Ⓐ knock down

Ⓑ from the ceiling

Ⓒ swung loosely

3 Which word from the passage has about the SAME meaning as *weary*?

Ⓐ sod

Ⓑ tired

Ⓒ big

GO ON →

Name: _____ Date: _____

4 Which statement BEST shows how Mama feels about living in a sod house?

Ⓐ Many people do not live as comfortably as her family.

Ⓑ Wooden houses have more problems than sod houses.

Ⓒ Life was better when the family had lived in the dugout.

5 Which sentence from the passage gives a clue about the meaning of *version*?

Ⓐ She drew a picture on the slate chalkboard she used for school.

Ⓑ She imagined what the new type of house would look like inside.

Ⓒ She hoped her mama could come live in it with her.

6 What does Mama mean when she says, "All things in good time"?

Ⓐ Everything should be in its proper place.

Ⓑ Some places are more fun to live than others.

Ⓒ People must be patient for changes to come.

7 With which idea would Louisa MOST LIKELY agree?

Ⓐ Modern things can make life easier.

Ⓑ It is important to remember the past.

Ⓒ It is better to fix things than throw them out.

GO ON →

**Read "Local Government at Work" before you answer
Numbers 8 through 15.**

Local Government at Work

Dale wants a place where her dog can run loose
and play with other dogs. A dog park is just what her
town needs, she decides. So Dale talks to her neighbors.
Many of them like her idea. But what is the next step?
Her dad tells her he knows of a place that can help her
make her idea happen.

Roles of Local Government

Dale and her dad go to their town hall, the offices
where local government works. The local government
helps people who live in a town. Town workers make sure
schools have money to run. They make sure firefighters and
police keep citizens safe. Town workers clean up parks and
fix streets. The town collects taxes to pay these workers.

Part of a Democracy

Local government is part of our **democracy**. As part of
this system, voters get to make some decisions. Dale learns
that each state makes the rules for local government. In her
state, voters choose a town mayor and town council.

Dale asks, "Could I be mayor someday?" Her dad
explains that long ago, only men could vote or hold office.
But the laws have since changed. As a result, now any
person over the age of 18 can vote or hold office.

GO ON →

Dale learns what she must do next. She writes a letter asking the town to create a dog park. She has to have several town citizens sign the letter. Her dad gives the letter to the selectmen. Voters will make the final decision at the town meeting.

How Town Meetings Work

Town meetings were first held in colonial times. Voters used the meetings to decide on new laws that everyone would follow. Dale lives in a state that still holds town meetings. Voters listen as people discuss new laws. Some laws tell how people may use public land. Some tell how to spend money collected from taxes.

Dale's dad helps explain her idea at the town meeting. People then discuss it and suggest **amendments**, or changes to the law. Then, they raise their hands to vote and someone counts the votes. The dog park is approved! Dale is proud to have a say in her local government. She is even happier that her dog now has a safe place to play.

The Town Meeting Process

1. A citizen requests a change in a law.

2. Citizens sign the request.

3. The request is printed in a warrant, or a list of items to be voted on.

4. People read the warrant to find out where and when the town meeting will be.

5. Voters vote on each request at the town meeting.

6. Approved requests become laws.

GO ON →

Name: _____ Date: _____

Use "Local Government at Work" to answer Numbers 8 through 15.

8 Dale and her dad go to the town hall because they want to _____.

Ⓐ have a dog park created in town

Ⓑ find out if dogs are allowed in town

Ⓒ learn how the town government works

9 Which sentence tells what local government must do to pay its workers?

Ⓐ The town gets citizens to sign letters.

Ⓑ The town schedules meetings.

Ⓒ The town collects taxes.

10 Which sentence from the article gives a clue about the meaning of *democracy*?

Ⓐ The local government helps people who live in a town.

Ⓑ As part of this system, voters get to make some decisions.

Ⓒ Dale learns that each state makes the rules for local government.

11 Which sentence in the article signals a cause-and-effect relationship?

Ⓐ Dale wants a place where her dog can run and play with other dogs.

Ⓑ Town workers make sure schools have money to run.

Ⓒ As a result, now any person over the age of 18 can vote or hold office.

12 Read this sentence from the article.

People then discuss it and suggest amendments, or changes to the law.

Which clue word in the sentence helps to explain what *amendments* means?

Ⓐ people

Ⓑ changes

Ⓒ law

13 Voters must raise their hands at a town meeting in order to _____.

Ⓐ vote for ideas

Ⓑ ask questions

Ⓒ discuss the laws

14 What will happen as a result of the vote at the town meeting?

Ⓐ The town will discuss whether to build a dog park.

Ⓑ The town will make plans to build a dog park.

Ⓒ The town will change laws inside dog parks.

15 According to the diagram, what must happen for a request to get printed in a warrant?

Ⓐ Citizens must sign the request.

Ⓑ Citizens must vote on the request.

Ⓒ Citizens must make the request a law.

STOP

Read "Casey Saves the Day" before you answer Numbers 1 through 7.

Casey Saves the Day

Did you ever hear the story of Casey Jones? Well, he was the finest railroad man who ever crossed the plains. Casey liked to run his train fast. Too fast, if you ask me.

When Casey's train passed by, the buffaloes looked at each other and wondered what it was. It sounded like a train and it smelled like a train, but it just looked like a silver flash.

How did he do it? "Pile on the black diamonds, boys," he yelled. Of course he meant coal, and plenty of it.

One morning, Casey jumped up and grabbed a rainbow on his way to work. It was going to be a special day. He could feel it in his bones.

"More coal, boys," he shouted. "I'm aiming to break a record today." He had the eyes of an eagle and never blinked. He was staring down the track several miles ahead when something caught his eye.

Now in those days, there were no crossing gates to keep folks safe. You just looked both ways, listened, and took your chances.

Some children were crossing the tracks on their way to school, and Casey saw them scatter to safety as the train approached. A little girl had her dog with her, but it didn't seem to want to budge. The poor thing just stood in place on the tracks, staring at Casey's train.

GO ON →

"Bob, take over!" Casey shouted to his buddy. "I'm going out. You slow this buggy down, fast as you can!"

Casey quickly made a lasso out of the rainbow he had put in his back pocket. Then he carefully inched forward to the front of the train. This was no time to feel **dizzy** and lose balance. Inch by inch, he moved forward. When he reached the front, the train had already slowed down quite a bit. Twirling his rainbow lasso, he tossed it at the dog's body and snatched the pup into the air.

"Hold on tight," he said gently as he held the dog and the train finally came to a stop.

Casey left the dog with the little girl, took off his hat, and gave a little bow. Then, he started up the engine again because he had a run to finish.

Now Casey was a man of action, not a man of **emotion**, but when he got home that day, he hugged his own sweet pup. Then he went and had himself a good cry.

GO ON →

Use "Casey Saves the Day" to answer Numbers 1 through 7.

1 How is Casey's train able to travel so fast?

Ⓐ Casey uses buffaloes.

Ⓑ Casey uses a lot of coal.

Ⓒ Casey uses a rainbow lasso.

2 Casey knows it is going to be a good day because he _____.

Ⓐ can feel it in his bones

Ⓑ has found black diamonds

Ⓒ is going to try to break a record

3 What is the MAIN problem in the passage?

Ⓐ A dog is on the tracks.

Ⓑ Casey must use a lasso.

Ⓒ The train is going too slow.

4 Which evidence from the text gives a clue about the meaning of *dizzy*?

Ⓐ inched forward

Ⓑ lose balance

Ⓒ tossed it

GO ON →

5 How does Casey solve his problem?

① He finds his sweet dog at home.

② He speeds up the train even more.

③ He uses the rainbow he grabbed earlier.

6 Why does Casey leave right AFTER he rescues the dog?

① He must finish his train run.

② He needs to get home to his dog.

③ He knows the dog will find its owner.

7 Read this sentence from the passage.

> **Now Casey was a man of action, not a man of emotion, but when he got home that day, he hugged his own sweet pup.**

Which sentence from the text gives a clue about the meaning of *emotion*?

① The poor thing just stood in place on the tracks, staring at Casey's train.

② Casey left the dog with the little girl, took off his hat, and gave a little bow.

③ Then he went and had himself a good cry.

Read "King Richard's Bones" before you answer Numbers 8 through 15.

King Richard's Bones

Scientists were excited to **uncover** an important skeleton. The bones were found under a parking lot in England. Experts spent months studying the bones. Finally, they came to a conclusion. The skeleton belonged to the long-lost king of England, King Richard III.

Who Was Richard III?

Richard became king in 1483. He was not born to be king. Instead he took the throne from his nephews. In 1485, Richard died on the battlefield at Bosworth. He was just 32 years old. No one knew where his body was buried until now.

Much of what we know about King Richard was learned from a play written by William Shakespeare. Shakespeare described Richard as being cruel. He also said that Richard had a curved spine. Other writers said the king was small and weak.

The Scientific Proof

Scientists looked at different kinds of evidence. They proved the bones belonged to Richard. First, they carefully examined the bones using magnifying tools such as a **microscope**. They could tell that this man had eaten a diet of meat and fish. In Richard's time, only the very rich could afford these foods.

It had been stated by people other than Shakespeare that Richard had a curved spine. The actual bones did have a curve that fit the description. Scientists then tested blood samples of people who were related to the king. There was a strong match to the bone material. That was the final proof they needed.

What the King Looked Like

An artist worked with the scientists. She used bones from the face and head to figure out what Richard looked like. People believed he had a mean and worried look. Old paintings show a man who looked very aged and wrinkled, as if he were about to **shrivel** up. The new model shows Richard looking young and healthy.

Scientists continue to look for more clues about King Richard III. Perhaps the paintings that hang in England will one day be repainted as more facts are revealed about this fascinating and mysterious ruler.

King Richard Discovered in England

Leicester
■ Where bones
were found
Bosworth ■
Battlefield
London ●

GO ON →

Use "King Richard's Bones" to answer Numbers 8 through 15.

8 Read these sentences from the article.

> **Scientists were excited to uncover an important skeleton. The bones were found under a parking lot in England.**

Which word from the sentences is a clue to the meaning of *uncover*?

Ⓐ excited

Ⓑ found

Ⓒ parking

9 How can you determine the order of events in the section "Who Was Richard III?"

Ⓐ by signal words in the text

Ⓑ by key dates listed in the text

Ⓒ by the description of Richard in the text

10 What problem did scientists have AFTER finding the bones?

Ⓐ They had no information about King Richard.

Ⓑ They did not know how King Richard had died.

Ⓒ They did not have proof that the bones belonged to King Richard.

11 What was the FIRST thing scientists did to connect the bones to Richard?

Ⓐ They read plays to learn about the shape of King Richard's body.

Ⓑ They tested blood samples against the bone material.

Ⓒ They examined the bones closely and carefully.

12 Which clue words from the article help to explain what *microscope* means?

Ⓐ kinds of evidence

Ⓑ magnifying tools

Ⓒ diet of meat and fish

13 Which sentence does NOT tell a way that the bones were identified?

Ⓐ An artist drew a picture of King Richard that made him look young.

Ⓑ Scientists compared the shape of the bones to descriptions from history.

Ⓒ Scientists tested blood samples of people who were distantly related to the king.

GO ON →

14 Read these sentences from the article.

> **Old paintings show a man who was very aged
> and wrinkled, as if he were about to shrivel up.
> The new model shows Richard looking young
> and healthy.**

Which phrase from the sentences helps you understand
the meaning of *shrivel*?

Ⓐ old paintings

Ⓑ aged and wrinkled

Ⓒ new model

15 According to the map, where were King Richard's
bones found?

Ⓐ on Bosworth Battlefield

Ⓑ near Leicester

Ⓒ in London

STOP

Read "The Old Violin" before you answer Numbers 1 through 7.

The Old Violin

In the months after World War II, Carl's life changed a lot. Carl's father came home from the army. He took a job in another state, and the family moved. Carl found himself living in an unfamiliar house in a new town. Carl **despised** the old house, but he appreciated the huge attic at the top of the stairs. It was filled with interesting objects left behind by past owners.

One day, Carl spotted a dusty case in the attic. He opened it and found an old violin inside. Carl showed the violin to his mother. He had always wanted to play a musical instrument. His mother agreed that he could keep the old violin and take lessons.

As the years passed, Carl became a very good musician. Even though he could afford a new instrument, he never bought another violin. The old violin from the attic had a beautiful sound. Carl tuned it himself. He expressed his **individuality** with the violin. His music sounded different each day, depending on his mood.

When Carl grew older, his hands began to shake and his fingers became stiff. His age made it difficult for him to play the violin. But still he wanted to hear its sound, so Carl began teaching his grandson, Jack, to play the instrument. Like Carl, Jack learned quickly. Soon, the boy was playing the old violin like an expert.

GO ON →

Carl's daughter was amazed at her son's musical talent. She wanted to make sure that Jack could continue to play the violin, so she took the instrument to a music shop to have it tuned. To her surprise, the owner of the shop offered her a large sum of money for the violin. As it turned out, the old instrument was very valuable.

Carl learned about the value of the violin from his daughter. She asked him if he wanted to sell the violin. As an answer, Carl handed the violin to his grandson. "The violin belongs to Jack now," he said. "He can sell it if he wants."

Jack looked at the old violin for a long time. Then he shook his head. "I'll never sell the violin," he said. "I'll play it as long as I can. Then I'll give it to one of my children to play."

And from that day on, playing the beautiful, old violin became a family tradition.

GO ON →

Use "The Old Violin" to answer Numbers 1 through 7.

1 Which word from the text means the OPPOSITE of *despised*?

Ⓐ unfamiliar

Ⓑ appreciated

Ⓒ interesting

2 Which sentence from the text tells why Carl never bought a new violin?

Ⓐ He could not afford a new violin.

Ⓑ His old violin had a beautiful sound.

Ⓒ He stopped playing the violin after a few years.

3 Which evidence from the passage gives a clue about the meaning of *individuality*?

Ⓐ As the years passed, Carl became a very good musician.

Ⓑ The old violin from the attic had a beautiful sound.

Ⓒ His music sounded different each day, depending on his mood.

4 Who does Carl teach to play the violin?

Ⓐ his son

Ⓑ his daughter

Ⓒ his grandson

5 What does Carl's daughter discover about the violin?

Ⓐ It is very valuable.

Ⓑ It needs to be tuned.

Ⓒ It belongs to someone else.

6 What does Jack decide to do with the old violin?

Ⓐ give it back to his grandfather

Ⓑ sell it and buy a new violin with the money

Ⓒ continue to play it and then give it to one of his children

7 What is the overall message of this passage?

Ⓐ Old things are better than new things.

Ⓑ Traditions can connect people to each other.

Ⓒ Valuable treasures can be found in old houses.

GO ON →

Read "Facts About Biofuels" before you answer Numbers 8 through 15.

Facts About Biofuels

Our class researched biofuels as a science project. We learned that biofuels are an important alternative, or different, energy source.

What Are Biofuels?

Biofuels are fuels made from plant or animal materials. Many of the biofuels we use today come from plants.

In the United States, we use corn to make a biofuel called ethanol. We mix ethanol with gasoline to power our cars and trucks. The country of Brazil also makes ethanol. Much of their ethanol is made from sugarcane.

There are other biofuels as well. Biofuels can be made from plant oils, such as palm oil or soybean oil.

The Benefits of Biofuels

Our research helped us understand that using biofuels can have **global** benefits. Biofuels can provide energy for countries around the world. Biofuels are also renewable fuel sources, meaning they can be made again and again. They are not limited. And biofuels may be better for the environment than coal and gasoline.

GO ON →

The Drawbacks of Biofuels

What are some **consequences**, or bad results, of creating biofuels? Our research showed that plants grown for biofuels often need fertilizers and pesticides. The farm equipment used to care for the plants may run on gasoline. The use of fertilizers, pesticides, and gasoline can pollute the environment. This is a drawback. In addition, biofuel plants take up valuable land that could be used to grow food crops.

The Future of Biofuels

To sum up our research, we learned that we must pay attention to the way biofuels are used today. Biofuels cannot be **ignored**. They have good points, such as the fact that they are renewable. They also have some drawbacks. One thing is certain. The discussion about biofuels needs to be continued.

Glossary

alternative (awl•TUR•nuh•tive) another choice or possibility

fertilizers (FUR•tuh•lyz•urz) materials put into the soil to help plants grow

fuel (FYOO•uhl) something used to create heat or power

pesticides (PEST•i•sidez) chemicals used to kill pests such as insects

GO ON →

Use "Facts About Biofuels" to answer Numbers 8 through 15.

8 What are biofuels made from?

   Ⓐ plant or animal materials

   Ⓑ coal and gasoline

   Ⓒ fertilizers and pesticides

9 Read this sentence from the article.

> **Our research helped us understand that using biofuels can have global benefits.**

Which phrase from the article gives a clue about the meaning of *global*?

   Ⓐ can be made

   Ⓑ such as palm oil

   Ⓒ around the world

10 Which detail from the text explains a benefit of biofuels?

   Ⓐ Biofuels are renewable.

   Ⓑ Biofuels are not food crops.

   Ⓒ Biofuels are an energy source.

GO ON →

11 Read this sentence from the article.

> **What are some consequences, or bad results, of creating biofuels?**

Which words from the sentence help to explain what *consequences* means?

(A) are some

(B) bad results

(C) creating biofuels

12 Which sentence from the text explains a drawback of biofuels?

(A) In the United States, we use corn to make a biofuel called ethanol.

(B) Biofuels can provide energy for countries around the world.

(C) In addition, biofuel plants take up valuable land that could be used to grow food crops.

13 Which term from the glossary is NOT an example of something that can pollute the environment?

(A) alternative

(B) fertilizers

(C) pesticides

GO ON →

Name: _____ Date: _____

Name: _____ **Date:** _____

14 Read this sentence from the article.

> **Biofuels cannot be ignored.**

Which words from the article mean almost the OPPOSITE of *ignored*?

Ⓐ sum up

Ⓑ pay attention

Ⓒ good points

15 What is the MAIN idea of this article?

Ⓐ Biofuels are not a good energy source.

Ⓑ Biofuels should be used throughout the world.

Ⓒ Biofuels are an important alternative energy source.

STOP

Fluency
Assessment

Our Great Forests

Long ago, most of the eastern United States was a big forest. The land was covered with trees. Today big parts of this forest are gone. People cut down the trees as they moved west. They used the trees to make farms and cities. Now people plant new forests. They want to put back some of the trees that were cut down.

There are three kinds of forests in the United States. In one kind the trees lose their leaves in the fall. In a second kind, the trees stay green all year. The third kind is a mixed forest. It has trees that lose their leaves and trees that stay green.

If you visit a forest, look at the trees. See if you can tell what kind they are.

👆 Why are people planting new forests?

👆 What are two types of forest in the United States?

Name: _____ Date: _____

Our Great Forests

11	Long ago, most of the eastern United States was a big
21	forest. The land was covered with trees. Today big parts
33	of this forest are gone. People cut down the trees as they
44	moved west. They used the trees to make farms and cities.
55	Now people plant new forests. They want to put back some
62	of the trees that were cut down.
72	There are three kinds of forests in the United States.
86	In one kind the trees lose their leaves in the fall. In a second
98	kind, the trees stay green all year. The third kind is a
110	mixed forest. It has trees that lose their leaves and trees that
112	stay green.
126	If you visit a forest, look at the trees. See if you can tell
130	what kind they are.

✓ Why are people planting new forests?

✓ What are two types of forest in the United States?

Words Read	–	Errors	=	WCPM

☐ **Fall (94 WCPM)**
☐ **Winter (112 WCPM)**
☐ **Spring (123 WCPM)**

WCPM	/	Words Read	=	Accuracy %

PROSODY	L1	L2	L3	L4
Reading in Phrases	O	O	O	O
Pace	O	O	O	O
Syntax	O	O	O	O
Self-correction	O	O	O	O
Intonation	O	O	O	O

Working Dogs

Dogs make wonderful pets. They are fun to play with, and they can be very friendly as well. But did you know that dogs can have jobs, too? Many dogs work. They help people in important ways.

Some dogs are trained to help blind people get around. They are called seeing-eye dogs. Other dogs are trained to help deaf people. They can alert their owners to sounds. The sound may be a fire alarm or a doorbell.

Most dogs have an excellent sense of smell. That is why police officers use them to locate people who are lost or hurt. Dogs also herd animals. They know how to make sheep and cows move along. They help to protect the animals as well. Even though dogs like to play, they are hard workers, too!

✔ What are "seeing-eye dogs"?

✔ Name two types of jobs dogs can have.

Name: _____ Date: _____

Working Dogs

10	Dogs make wonderful pets. They are fun to play with,
22	and they can be very friendly as well. But did you know
33	that dogs can have jobs, too? Many dogs work. They help
37	people in important ways.
47	Some dogs are trained to help blind people get around.
58	They are called seeing-eye dogs. Other dogs are trained to
68	help deaf people. They can alert their owners to sounds.
78	The sound may be a fire alarm or a doorbell.
89	Most dogs have an excellent sense of smell. That is why
100	police officers use them to locate people who are lost or
110	hurt. Dogs also herd animals. They know how to make
120	sheep and cows move along. They help to protect the
131	animals as well. Even though dogs like to play, they are
134	hard workers, too!

✔ What are "seeing-eye dogs"?

✔ Name two types of jobs dogs can have.

Words Read	–	Errors	=	WCPM

☐ **Fall (94 WCPM)**
☐ **Winter (112 WCPM)**
☐ **Spring (123 WCPM)**

WCPM	/	Words Read	=	Accuracy %

PROSODY				
	L1	L2	L3	L4
Reading in Phrases	O	O	O	O
Pace	O	O	O	O
Syntax	O	O	O	O
Self-correction	O	O	O	O
Intonation	O	O	O	O

Kurt Goes to School

Mark had a playful dog named Kurt. Kurt was a nice dog, but he had a problem. He disturbed people when they were eating by putting his paws on the table and barking.

"Kurt will have to go to dog school," Mark's father declared.

Kurt had to stay at the school for three days. Mark missed him. He could not wait until Kurt would come home.

Finally, Mark and his dad went to pick up Kurt. While they ate lunch, Kurt sat quietly. He did not put his paws on the table. He did not bark.

Mark's father noted, "See, Mark. Kurt is now a well-behaved dog." Mark was just happy to have his furry pal back.

When they got home, Mark talked to Kurt. "From now on, I'm the only one who goes to school," he said. Kurt wagged his tail.

✔ What is Kurt's problem?

✔ How does Mark's dad solve the problem?

Name: _____ Date: _____

Kurt Goes to School

11	Mark had a playful dog named Kurt. Kurt was a nice
22	dog, but he had a problem. He disturbed people when they
33	were eating by putting his paws on the table and barking.
43	"Kurt will have to go to dog school," Mark's father
44	declared.
55	Kurt had to stay at the school for three days. Mark
65	missed him. He could not wait until Kurt would come
66	home.
77	Finally, Mark and his dad went to pick up Kurt. While
90	they ate lunch, Kurt sat quietly. He did not put his paws on
96	the table. He did not bark.
105	Mark's father noted, "See, Mark. Kurt is now a
116	well-behaved dog." Mark was just happy to have his furry
118	pal back.
128	When they got home, Mark talked to Kurt. "From now
140	on, I'm the only one who goes to school," he said. Kurt
143	wagged his tail.

 What is Kurt's problem?

 How does Mark's dad solve the problem?

Words Read	–	Errors	=	WCPM

☐ **Fall (94 WCPM)**
☐ **Winter (112 WCPM)**
☐ **Spring (123 WCPM)**

WCPM	/	Words Read	=	Accuracy %

PROSODY				
	L1	L2	L3	L4
Reading in Phrases	O	O	O	O
Pace	O	O	O	O
Syntax	O	O	O	O
Self-correction	O	O	O	O
Intonation	O	O	O	O

Slow as a Sloth

Sloths live in the rainforests of Central and South America. They are very slow moving. They may stay in the same tree for most of their lives. They can live for 30 years. They do not need much food because they are so slow. Sloths eat fruit, buds, and twigs.

There are two types of sloths. One has two toes on each foot. The other type has three toes. They are about the size of a small dog. Their fur is gray and brown. Their faces look like they are smiling.

Their long arms and big claws help them hang from branches. Sloths may sleep for as long as 20 hours a day. While sleeping, they put their heads between their arms. This helps to hide them from predators. At night they are awake, looking for food.

✔ Where do sloths live?

✔ Why do sloths eat so little?

Name: _____ Date: _____

Slow as a Sloth

9	Sloths live in the rainforests of Central and South
20	America. They are very slow moving. They may stay in the
33	same tree for most of their lives. They can live for 30 years.
44	They do not need much food because they are so slow.
50	Sloths eat fruit, buds, and twigs.
62	There are two types of sloths. One has two toes on each
74	foot. The other type has three toes. They are about the size
87	of a small dog. Their fur is gray and brown. Their faces look
91	like they are smiling.
101	Their long arms and big claws help them hang from
113	branches. Sloths may sleep for as long as 20 hours a day.
122	While sleeping, they put their heads between their arms.
133	This helps to hide them from predators. At night they are
137	awake, looking for food.

✓ Where do sloths live?

✓ Why do sloths eat so little?

Words Read	–	Errors	=	WCPM

☐ **Fall (94 WCPM)**
☐ **Winter (112 WCPM)**
☐ **Spring (123 WCPM)**

WCPM	/	Words Read	=	Accuracy %

PROSODY				
	L1	L2	L3	L4
Reading in Phrases	O	O	O	O
Pace	O	O	O	O
Syntax	O	O	O	O
Self-correction	O	O	O	O
Intonation	O	O	O	O

Why Do Zebras Have Stripes?

Herds of zebras are found on the plains of Africa. They look like small horses. In fact, they are related to horses. But they do not have the colors of horses we know. Instead, they have stripes that are black and white. Every zebra has its own design.

Stripes help keep zebras cool. They also help to protect the animals. How? When zebras stand in a herd, their stripes seem to blend together. This makes it hard for a lion. It cannot see just one zebra. The herd may look like one big blob.

There are three types of zebras. Each type has stripes that are a little different. One kind has wide stripes that fade to gray. A second kind has narrow stripes. The third kind has white stripes that look more like the color of cream.

✔ What animal does a zebra look like?

✔ How do its stripes help the zebra?

Name: _____ Date: _____

Why Do Zebras Have Stripes?

11	Herds of zebras are found on the plains of Africa. They
23	look like small horses. In fact, they are related to horses. But
35	they do not have the colors of horses we know. Instead, they
46	have stripes that are black and white. Every zebra has its
48	own design.
58	Stripes help keep zebras cool. They also help to protect
68	the animals. How? When zebras stand in a herd, their
80	stripes seem to blend together. This makes it hard for a lion.
92	It cannot see just one zebra. The herd may look like one
94	big blob.
105	There are three types of zebras. Each type has stripes that
117	are a little different. One kind has wide stripes that fade to
128	gray. A second kind has narrow stripes. The third kind has
138	white stripes that look more like the color of cream.

✔ What animal does a zebra look like?

✔ How do its stripes help the zebra?

Words Read	–	Errors	=	WCPM

☐ Fall (94 WCPM)
☐ Winter (112 WCPM)
☐ Spring (123 WCPM)

WCPM	/	Words Read	=	Accuracy %

PROSODY				
	L1	L2	L3	L4
Reading in Phrases	O	O	O	O
Pace	O	O	O	O
Syntax	O	O	O	O
Self-correction	O	O	O	O
Intonation	O	O	O	O

Phillip Steps Up

Phillip Palmer was a quiet student. He completed his work and got good grades, but he just never had much to say.

One day, Phillip's class was working in groups on different projects. A boy in his group said to another boy, "That's not the way to do it. Why can't you do it the right way?" His voice sounded mean and nasty.

Phillip became angry. "You are being a bully," he said to the boy. "You cannot treat people that way because we have learned to respect and help each other."

The boy was surprised since no student had ever talked to him that way. He wanted to say something mean to Phillip. But he stopped when he saw his fierce and determined face.

"I'm sorry," said the boy. He was more respectful the rest of the time.

👆 What upsets Phillip?

👆 How does Phillip help a classmate?

Name: _____ Date: _____

Phillip Steps Up

9	Phillip Palmer was a quiet student. He completed his
20	work and got good grades, but he just never had much
22	to say.
31	One day, Phillip's class was working in groups on
42	different projects. A boy in his group said to another boy,
56	"That's not the way to do it. Why can't you do it the right
63	way?" His voice sounded mean and nasty.
74	Phillip became angry. "You are being a bully," he said to
85	the boy. "You cannot treat people that way because we have
92	learned to respect and help each other."
102	The boy was surprised since no student had ever talked
113	to him that way. He wanted to say something mean to
123	Phillip. But he stopped when he saw his fierce and
125	determined face.
136	"I'm sorry," said the boy. He was more respectful the rest
139	of the time.

 What upsets Phillip?

 How does Phillip help a classmate?

Words Read	–	Errors	=	WCPM

☐ **Fall (94 WCPM)**
☐ **Winter (112 WCPM)**
☐ **Spring (123 WCPM)**

WCPM	/	Words Read	=	Accuracy %

PROSODY				
	L1	L2	L3	L4
Reading in Phrases	O	O	O	O
Pace	O	O	O	O
Syntax	O	O	O	O
Self-correction	O	O	O	O
Intonation	O	O	O	O

Flood Rescue

Jack, his mother, and sister watched as rain fell in torrents. Since they lived at the top of a steep hill, Jack's family was lucky

"Cory's family lives right near the stream!" cried Jack. "Can we help them?" he asked.

"Of course," said Jack's mom. "Luckily my cell phone is working, and I can call them right now."

It wasn't long before Cory's family was knocking at the door. They were soaking wet and were glad to get into some dry clothes. Soon it was time for bed.

From his window, Jack watched the storm. Soon, the whole house was quiet.

Jack woke up early. He looked out the window and down the hill. He saw that the stream had flooded. Just then he heard the sound of motorboats.

"Phew!" said Jack. "Looks like everyone will be rescued."

✔ Why is Jack's family safe from the storm?

✔ Why is Jack worried about Cory's family?

Name: _____ Date: _____

Flood Rescue

10	Jack, his mother, and sister watched as rain fell in
22	torrents. Since they lived at the top of a steep hill, Jack's
25	family was lucky
34	"Cory's family lives right near the stream!" cried Jack.
40	"Can we help them?" he asked.
50	"Of course," said Jack's mom. "Luckily my cell phone is
58	working, and I can call them right now."
68	It wasn't long before Cory's family was knocking at the
80	door. They were soaking wet and were glad to get into some
88	dry clothes. Soon it was time for bed.
97	From his window, Jack watched the storm. Soon, the
101	whole house was quiet.
112	Jack woke up early. He looked out the window and down
124	the hill. He saw that the stream had flooded. Just then he
129	heard the sound of motorboats.
138	"Phew!" said Jack. "Looks like everyone will be rescued."

✓ Why is Jack's family safe from the storm?

✓ Why is Jack worried about Cory's family?

Words Read	−	Errors	=	WCPM

☐ **Fall (94 WCPM)**
☐ **Winter (112 WCPM)**
☐ **Spring (123 WCPM)**

WCPM	/	Words Read	=	Accuracy %

PROSODY			
	L1	L2	L3	L4
Reading in Phrases	O	O	O	O
Pace	O	O	O	O
Syntax	O	O	O	O
Self-correction	O	O	O	O
Intonation	O	O	O	O

Learning Something New

The program Amy watched in class was amazing. She never knew how important bats were. She discovered that bats help to pollinate flowers. They also eat tons of insects that damage crops and harm people. Bats were now Amy's new favorite animal.

That weekend Amy was at a picnic and heard people talking about bats.

"They are ugly and dangerous pests," one woman said. "They should be destroyed." Amy was upset when other people agreed with the woman. She had to say something.

"Bats are helpful," Amy said. "You don't see many mosquitoes bothering us at this picnic. That's because bats live around here. They eat insects at night. They won't bite you either. If they fly close to you, they will just dart away. They are chasing a tasty bug."

Amy was able to change their opinions about bats.

👆 What animal is Amy interested in?

👆 What does Amy do at the picnic?

Name: _____ Date: _____

Learning Something New

9	The program Amy watched in class was amazing. She
18	never knew how important bats were. She discovered that
29	bats help to pollinate flowers. They also eat tons of insects
39	that damage crops and harm people. Bats were now Amy's
42	new favorite animal.
52	That weekend Amy was at a picnic and heard people
55	talking about bats.
64	"They are ugly and dangerous pests," one woman said.
73	"They should be destroyed." Amy was upset when other
83	people agreed with the woman. She had to say something.
92	"Bats are helpful," Amy said. "You don't see many
101	mosquitoes bothering us at this picnic. That's because bats
112	live around here. They eat insects at night. They won't bite
125	you either. If they fly close to you, they will just dart away.
131	They are chasing a tasty bug."
140	Amy was able to change their opinions about bats.

✔ What animal is Amy interested in?

✔ What does Amy do at the picnic?

Words Read	–	Errors	=	WCPM

☐ **Fall (94 WCPM)**
☐ **Winter (112 WCPM)**
☐ **Spring (123 WCPM)**

WCPM	/	Words Read	=	Accuracy %

PROSODY				
	L1	L2	L3	L4
Reading in Phrases	O	O	O	O
Pace	O	O	O	O
Syntax	O	O	O	O
Self-correction	O	O	O	O
Intonation	O	O	O	O

Greyhounds

Greyhounds are dogs that can run very fast. Some of them run in races. Most greyhounds can race for just a few years. Then homes must be found for them. Special groups help them find homes.

A group that helps greyhounds find homes is called an *adoption group*. There are adoption groups for all kinds of dogs and cats. There are even groups for horses.

The people who help in these groups love animals. They are hopeful that each one will find a good home. They want to make sure the homes give good care.

Sometimes it is hard to find homes for greyhounds. They are cute but big. Many of them grow up on a racetrack. (In some states, greyhound racing is an organized sport.) They have never lived in a home. They have not lived with a family. Some adoption groups work with the greyhounds. They help them get ready to live in a home.

👆 How long can greyhounds be racing dogs?

👆 Why can it be difficult to find homes for greyhounds?

Name: _____ Date: _____

Greyhounds

10	Greyhounds are dogs that can run very fast. Some of
22	them run in races. Most greyhounds can race for just a few
32	years. Then homes must be found for them. Special groups
36	help them find homes.
46	A group that helps greyhounds find homes is called an
56	*adoption group*. There are adoption groups for all kinds of
65	dogs and cats. There are even groups for horses.
75	The people who help in these groups love animals. They
87	are hopeful that each one will find a good home. They want
95	to make sure the homes give good care.
104	Sometimes it is hard to find homes for greyhounds.
117	They are cute but big. Many of them grow up on a racetrack.
126	(In some states, greyhound racing is an organized sport.)
138	They have never lived in a home. They have not lived with
147	a family. Some adoption groups work with the greyhounds.
157	They help them get ready to live in a home.

 How long can greyhounds be racing dogs?

 Why can it be difficult to find homes for greyhounds?

Words Read	–	Errors	=	WCPM

☐ **Fall (94 WCPM)**
☐ **Winter (112 WCPM)**
☐ **Spring (123 WCPM)**

WCPM	/	Words Read	=	Accuracy %

PROSODY				
	L1	L2	L3	L4
Reading in Phrases	O	O	O	O
Pace	O	O	O	O
Syntax	O	O	O	O
Self-correction	O	O	O	O
Intonation	O	O	O	O

Space Age Science

The space program is exciting. Astronauts have visited the moon. They have gone around Earth many times in the shuttle. They also have helped build the space station. The space program has allowed us to explore Mars and other planets.

Many people like the space program. However, they wonder what it does for them. In fact, the space program is a part of many things. Some are things we use everyday. To send people into space, scientists had to create new technology. The new tools and products they made helped astronauts live in space. They also helped people on Earth.

Solar panels came from the space program. Freeze-dried food and water filters did as well. We have power tools without cords because of the space program. Equipment made for astronauts also has helped fight fires on Earth. The computer mouse came from the space program, too. We can thank the space program for making long-distance phone calls easier as well.

👆 Why does the author view the space program as "exciting"?

👆 How does the space program help people on Earth?

Name: _____ Date: _____

Space Age Science

8	The space program is exciting. Astronauts have visited
19	the moon. They have gone around Earth many times in the
28	shuttle. They also have helped build the space station.
38	The space program has allowed us to explore Mars and
40	other planets.
48	Many people like the space program. However, they
60	wonder what it does for them. In fact, the space program is
71	a part of many things. Some are things we use everyday.
81	To send people into space, scientists had to create new
90	technology. The new tools and products they made helped
100	astronauts live in space. They also helped people on Earth.
109	Solar panels came from the space program. Freeze-dried
120	food and water filters did as well. We have power tools
128	without cords because of the space program. Equipment
138	made for astronauts also has helped fight fires on Earth.
147	The computer mouse came from the space program, too.
157	We can thank the space program for making long-distance
162	phone calls easier as well.

✓ Why does the author view the space program as "exciting"?

✓ How does the space program help people on Earth?

Words Read	–	Errors	=	WCPM

☐ **Fall (94 WCPM)**
☐ **Winter (112 WCPM)**
☐ **Spring (123 WCPM)**

WCPM	/	Words Read	=	Accuracy %

PROSODY				
	L1	L2	L3	L4
Reading in Phrases	O	O	O	O
Pace	O	O	O	O
Syntax	O	O	O	O
Self-correction	O	O	O	O
Intonation	O	O	O	O

The Welcome Club

Kevin and Ally noticed that their town was becoming bigger. More people were moving in. "There are two new families in my neighborhood," Kevin said. "And I see new faces at school."

"Some of the kids are from other countries," Ally added. "It must be hard to learn a new language. It's hard enough being in a new school."

"I have an idea," Kevin said. "Let's see how we can help the new kids." And that is how the Welcome Club was born.

Kevin and Ally talked to their friends. Many of them wanted to help. They talked to their teacher. Then their principal helped them with a plan. When new students were about to start school, the principal informed the Welcome Club. The club ate lunch with them. They took them on a tour. They answered questions and helped them find places. The Welcome Club became the new students' first friends.

👆 What is the Welcome Club?

👆 How does Kevin and Ally's principal help the Welcome Club?

Name: _____ Date: _____

The Welcome Club

9	Kevin and Ally noticed that their town was becoming
19	bigger. More people were moving in. "There are two new
29	families in my neighborhood," Kevin said. "And I see new
32	faces at school."
42	"Some of the kids are from other countries," Ally added.
54	"It must be hard to learn a new language. It's hard enough
59	being in a new school."
71	"I have an idea," Kevin said. "Let's see how we can help
83	the new kids." And that is how the Welcome Club was born.
93	Kevin and Ally talked to their friends. Many of them
103	wanted to help. They talked to their teacher. Then their
113	principal helped them with a plan. When new students were
122	about to start school, the principal informed the Welcome
134	Club. The club ate lunch with them. They took them on a
143	tour. They answered questions and helped them find places.
152	The Welcome Club became the new students' first friends.

 What is the Welcome Club?

 How does Kevin and Ally's principal help the Welcome Club?

Words Read	–	Errors	=	WCPM

☐ **Fall (94 WCPM)**
☐ **Winter (112 WCPM)**
☐ **Spring (123 WCPM)**

WCPM	/	Words Read	=	Accuracy %

PROSODY				
	L1	L2	L3	L4
Reading in Phrases	O	O	O	O
Pace	O	O	O	O
Syntax	O	O	O	O
Self-correction	O	O	O	O
Intonation	O	O	O	O

The Campaign

Tyra thought that the school elections were silly. Three students wanted to be president of the fourth grade. Posters were going up in the halls. Many students were wearing paper tags that read "Vote For" with a name written in.

The candidates also were telling students why they should be president. Tyra had not heard one good reason from any of them. One candidate wanted shorter school days. Another wanted more options during lunch. The third promised no homework if elected.

"None of them have the power to fulfill any of these promises," Tyra muttered. "We need a serious candidate." And suddenly that candidate became Tyra.

Tyra told others she wanted to make a difference. She wanted to start a recycling program in school. She wanted to partner with other schools to find ways to help their community. Tyra did not think that anyone would take her seriously. But they did. Tyra was soon the class president.

☑ Why does Tyra think none of the candidates are serious?

☑ Who wins the fourth-grade election?

Name: _____   Date: _____

The Campaign

9	Tyra thought that the school elections were silly. Three
19	students wanted to be president of the fourth grade. Posters
29	were going up in the halls. Many students were wearing
40	paper tags that read "Vote For" with a name written in.
48	The candidates also were telling students why they
58	should be president. Tyra had not heard one good reason
67	from any of them. One candidate wanted shorter school
76	days. Another wanted more options during lunch. The third
81	promised no homework if elected.
92	"None of them have the power to fulfill any of these
100	promises," Tyra muttered. "We need a serious candidate."
106	And suddenly that candidate became Tyra.
116	Tyra told others she wanted to make a difference. She
126	wanted to start a recycling program in school. She wanted
137	to partner with other schools to find ways to help their
147	community. Tyra did not think that anyone would take her
157	seriously. But they did. Tyra was soon the class president.

✔ Why does Tyra think none of the candidates are serious?

✔ Who wins the fourth-grade election?

Words Read	–	Errors	=	WCPM

☐ **Fall (94 WCPM)**
☐ **Winter (112 WCPM)**
☐ **Spring (123 WCPM)**

WCPM	/	Words Read	=	Accuracy %

PROSODY				
	L1	L2	L3	L4
Reading in Phrases	O	O	O	O
Pace	O	O	O	O
Syntax	O	O	O	O
Self-correction	O	O	O	O
Intonation	O	O	O	O

Moon Mysteries

The moon is the biggest (and most familiar) object in our night sky. But how much do we really know about the moon? Throughout history, people have made up stories about the moon, but most are not true. For example, there is no "man in the moon." The face we think we see is formed by shadows on mountains and in craters.

Over many years, we have learned a lot about our moon. Many scientists think the moon was formed from Earth. It happened millions of years ago. An object about the size of Mars hit Earth when it was still forming. The material knocked off from Earth became the moon. Once in orbit, the moon's gravity helped stop Earth from wobbling.

Although the moon is dry, scientists now think there is water on the moon. A spacecraft sent to the moon detected water vapor. This may come from ice deep in dark craters.

What is the "man in the moon"?

What theory do scientists have about the moon's creation?

Name: _____ Date: _____

Moon Mysteries

11	The moon is the biggest (and most familiar) object in our
22	night sky. But how much do we really know about the
30	moon? Throughout history, people have made up stories
42	about the moon, but most are not true. For example, there is
55	no "man in the moon." The face we think we see is formed
62	by shadows on mountains and in craters.
73	Over many years, we have learned a lot about our moon.
83	Many scientists think the moon was formed from Earth. It
94	happened millions of years ago. An object about the size of
104	Mars hit Earth when it was still forming. The material
115	knocked off from Earth became the moon. Once in orbit, the
122	moon's gravity helped stop Earth from wobbling.
132	Although the moon is dry, scientists now think there is
143	water on the moon. A spacecraft sent to the moon detected
154	water vapor. This may come from ice deep in dark craters.

✔ What is the "man in the moon"?

✔ What theory do scientists have about the moon's creation?

Words Read	–	Errors	=	WCPM

☐ **Fall (94 WCPM)**
☐ **Winter (112 WCPM)**
☐ **Spring (123 WCPM)**

WCPM	/	Words Read	=	Accuracy %

PROSODY				
	L1	L2	L3	L4
Reading in Phrases	O	O	O	O
Pace	O	O	O	O
Syntax	O	O	O	O
Self-correction	O	O	O	O
Intonation	O	O	O	O

Wrong Number

Mr. Bayville did not like telephones. In particular, he disliked cell phones. He certainly did not think they were "smart" phones. "Cell phones are dangerous," he would say. Then he would say that people crashed their cars because of cell phones. Or that people walked into walls because of cell phones.

At the library, Mr. Bayville read about the invention of the telephone. He read about Alexander Graham Bell's first phone call. Bell had called his assistant Thomas Watson from another room. His first words were, "Mr. Watson, come here. I want to see you."

To get rid of the telephone, Mr. Bayville built a one-person time machine. He set the clock for March 10, 1876, and climbed in. The machine whirred and shook. In just a few moments, Mr. Bayville was in the room with Mr. Watson. Over the wire, Bell's voice could be heard, calling for Mr. Watson.

"Don't answer that call," Mr. Bayville shouted. "It's a wrong number."

👆 What does Mr. Bayville dislike?

👆 What text evidence proves this story is not realistic?

Name: _____ Date: _____

Wrong Number

9	Mr. Bayville did not like telephones. In particular, he
19	disliked cell phones. He certainly did not think they were
27	"smart" phones. "Cell phones are dangerous," he would
37	say. Then he would say that people crashed their cars
47	because of cell phones. Or that people walked into walls
51	because of cell phones.
61	At the library, Mr. Bayville read about the invention of
70	the telephone. He read about Alexander Graham Bell's first
79	phone call. Bell had called his assistant Thomas Watson
88	from another room. His first words were, "Mr. Watson,
95	come here. I want to see you."
105	To get rid of the telephone, Mr. Bayville built a
116	one-person time machine. He set the clock for March 10,
125	1876, and climbed in. The machine whirred and shook.
137	In just a few moments, Mr. Bayville was in the room with
147	Mr. Watson. Over the wire, Bell's voice could be heard,
151	calling for Mr. Watson.
160	"Don't answer that call," Mr. Bayville shouted. "It's a
162	wrong number."

✔ What does Mr. Bayville dislike?

✔ What text evidence proves this story is not realistic?

Words Read	–	Errors	=	WCPM

☐ **Fall (94 WCPM)**
☐ **Winter (112 WCPM)**
☐ **Spring (123 WCPM)**

WCPM	/	Words Read	=	Accuracy %

PROSODY				
	L1	L2	L3	L4
Reading in Phrases	O	O	O	O
Pace	O	O	O	O
Syntax	O	O	O	O
Self-correction	O	O	O	O
Intonation	O	O	O	O

Ancient Farming

The Andes mountains of Peru are changing. Weather patterns are more extreme. Farmers who live high in the mountains find it hard to grow crops in the ways they are used to. So, many farmers are looking to the past.

Hundreds of years ago farmers in the Andes grew their crops on mounds of earth. The crops were watered with canals. The ruins of the canals can be seen still. Farmers are now repairing the canals. They are building up the mounds. In some places where the old ways are being used, crops have increased.

The farmers are also planting some of the crops their ancestors grew. These plants are stronger. They grow better in the highest parts of the mountains. The plants will grow in spite of frost, floods, and drought. One of these crops is a small pink potato. The potatoes can be stored for up to two years. Then, they still can be eaten.

✔ How are the Andes changing?

✔ How did farmers in the Andes change their methods?

Name: _____   Date: _____

Ancient Farming

8	The Andes mountains of Peru are changing. Weather
18	patterns are more extreme. Farmers who live high in the
30	mountains find it hard to grow crops in the ways they are
40	used to. So, many farmers are looking to the past.
50	Hundreds of years ago farmers in the Andes grew their
60	crops on mounds of earth. The crops were watered with
72	canals. The ruins of the canals can be seen still. Farmers are
82	now repairing the canals. They are building up the mounds.
93	In some places where the old ways are being used, crops
95	have increased.
105	The farmers are also planting some of the crops their
114	ancestors grew. These plants are stronger. They grow better
125	in the highest parts of the mountains. The plants will grow
138	in spite of frost, floods, and drought. One of these crops is a
150	small pink potato. The potatoes can be stored for up to two
157	years. Then, they still can be eaten.

✓ How are the Andes changing?

✓ How did farmers in the Andes change their methods?

Words Read	–	Errors	=	WCPM

☐ **Fall (94 WCPM)**
☐ **Winter (112 WCPM)**
☐ **Spring (123 WCPM)**

WCPM	/	Words Read	=	Accuracy %

PROSODY				
	L1	L2	L3	L4
Reading in Phrases	O	O	O	O
Pace	O	O	O	O
Syntax	O	O	O	O
Self-correction	O	O	O	O
Intonation	O	O	O	O

Not Interested

Joel entered his new school and looked for his classroom. He had seen the school a couple of weeks ago when he had come to register with his dad. He liked what he saw because there were students from many different backgrounds. They all seemed to be really involved in their school.

In his class, Joel saw the familiar things. Some students were quiet while others liked to joke around. Some had little trouble with the work and some struggled. And he noticed that most were friendly, but there was always at least one kid who was not.

He met this kid at lunch. Because he was new, the kid thought Joel was an easy target. He made fun of Joel's clothes and the way he wore his hair. He made fun of Joel's old school, too.

Joel sighed. Having moved a lot, he was used to it. Joel stared at the kid for a long moment. Then he said, "I'm not interested."

👆 What new situation is Joel dealing with?

👆 What does Joel mean when he says he is "not interested"?

Name: _____ Date: _____

Not Interested

10	Joel entered his new school and looked for his classroom.
23	He had seen the school a couple of weeks ago when he had
35	come to register with his dad. He liked what he saw because
43	there were students from many different backgrounds. They
52	all seemed to be really involved in their school.
62	In his class, Joel saw the familiar things. Some students
73	were quiet while others liked to joke around. Some had little
83	trouble with the work and some struggled. And he noticed
94	that most were friendly, but there was always at least one
98	kid who was not.
110	He met this kid at lunch. Because he was new, the kid
121	thought Joel was an easy target. He made fun of Joel's
134	clothes and the way he wore his hair. He made fun of Joel's
137	old school, too.
148	Joel sighed. Having moved a lot, he was used to it.
160	Joel stared at the kid for a long moment. Then he said,
163	"I'm not interested."

✔ What new situation is Joel dealing with?

✔ What does Joel mean when he says he is "not interested"?

Words Read	–	Errors	=	WCPM

☐ **Fall (94 WCPM)**
☐ **Winter (112 WCPM)**
☐ **Spring (123 WCPM)**

WCPM	/	Words Read	=	Accuracy %

PROSODY				
	L1	L2	L3	L4
Reading in Phrases	O	O	O	O
Pace	O	O	O	O
Syntax	O	O	O	O
Self-correction	O	O	O	O
Intonation	O	O	O	O

Wildlife and the Bay

Many animals live in and around the bay not far from my town. We live on the Oregon coast. The blue sea makes a fine home for wildlife. Tiny and big fish live in the water, along with crabs and sea stars. Even small sharks swim along the shore. Mammals such as sea otters live there too. Birds cluster on the rocky cliffs above the bay.

The sea otters are strong swimmers and divers. They make their homes on the shore. But they spend most of their time in the water. Sea otters eat fish, mussels, and clams. It's fun to watch them crack open clams with rocks. They use their stomachs as a dining table. After a meal, they spend a long time cleaning their faces and whiskers.

Eagles make their homes on the cliffs above the bay. They lay their eggs in large nests made of sticks. After the eggs hatch, the mother and father leave the chicks. They fly off to catch fish for their babies.

✔ Where does the narrator live?

✔ Where do sea otters spend most of their time?

Name: _____ Date: _____

Wildlife and the Bay

12	Many animals live in and around the bay not far from my
24	town. We live on the Oregon coast. The blue sea makes a
36	fine home for wildlife. Tiny and big fish live in the water,
46	along with crabs and sea stars. Even small sharks swim
57	along the shore. Mammals such as sea otters live there too.
66	Birds cluster on the rocky cliffs above the bay.
75	The sea otters are strong swimmers and divers. They
87	make their homes on the shore. But they spend most of their
99	time in the water. Sea otters eat fish, mussels, and clams. It's
110	fun to watch them crack open clams with rocks. They use
122	their stomachs as a dining table. After a meal, they spend a
129	long time cleaning their faces and whiskers.
140	Eagles make their homes on the cliffs above the bay. They
152	lay their eggs in large nests made of sticks. After the eggs
164	hatch, the mother and father leave the chicks. They fly off to
169	catch fish for their babies.

✔ Where does the narrator live?

✔ Where do sea otters spend most of their time?

Words Read	–	Errors	=	WCPM

☐ **Fall (94 WCPM)**
☐ **Winter (112 WCPM)**
☐ **Spring (123 WCPM)**

WCPM	/	Words Read	=	Accuracy %

PROSODY				
	L1	L2	L3	L4
Reading in Phrases	O	O	O	O
Pace	O	O	O	O
Syntax	O	O	O	O
Self-correction	O	O	O	O
Intonation	O	O	O	O

Snakes That Stay Off the Ground

Some people think that all snakes live on the ground. That is not true. Snakes can live in the water and up in trees, too.

Water snakes have lived in many places in the world. They often prey on fish and other animals that live in the same area. These snakes can swim just like fish. To defend themselves, water snakes will puff up their heads and open their mouths. This makes them look large and fierce. They also can give off a bad smell as a defense.

Some snakes live in trees. These green or brown snakes are difficult to see. Their color patterns blend in with the dappled leaves of the tree. Some tree snakes can be very small and thin. These snakes are able to blend in with vines growing on a tree. Other tree snakes can flatten themselves and glide from tree to tree. Tree snakes usually prey on birds and frogs.

So whenever you think about snakes, look up as well as down! Snakes are not always on the ground.

✔ Where can snakes live?

✔ How can water snakes protect themselves?

Name: _____ Date: _____

Snakes That Stay Off the Ground

10	Some people think that all snakes live on the ground.
23	That is not true. Snakes can live in the water and up in
25	trees, too.
35	Water snakes have lived in many places in the world.
47	They often prey on fish and other animals that live in the
58	same area. These snakes can swim just like fish. To defend
68	themselves, water snakes will puff up their heads and open
78	their mouths. This makes them look large and fierce. They
88	also can give off a bad smell as a defense.
98	Some snakes live in trees. These green or brown snakes
109	are difficult to see. Their color patterns blend in with the
120	dappled leaves of the tree. Some tree snakes can be very
132	small and thin. These snakes are able to blend in with vines
142	growing on a tree. Other tree snakes can flatten themselves
153	and glide from tree to tree. Tree snakes usually prey on
156	birds and frogs.
167	So whenever you think about snakes, look up as well as
175	down! Snakes are not always on the ground.

☑ Where can snakes live?

☑ How can water snakes protect themselves?

Words Read	–	Errors	=	WCPM

☐ **Fall (94 WCPM)**
☐ **Winter (112 WCPM)**
☐ **Spring (123 WCPM)**

WCPM	/	Words Read	=	Accuracy %

PROSODY				
	L1	L2	L3	L4
Reading in Phrases	O	O	O	O
Pace	O	O	O	O
Syntax	O	O	O	O
Self-correction	O	O	O	O
Intonation	O	O	O	O

The Photo Album

Maribel wanted to know about her family history. She knew her family originally came from Mexico. But she was not sure exactly where they had lived. Everyone seemed to be too busy to answer her questions. Some who did listen just said they didn't know.

On a weekend trip to see her aunt and uncle, there was a thunderstorm. It was too rainy to go outside, so Maribel decided to ask her aunt and uncle about her family history.

"Your great-grandmother and great-grandfather came from a little town outside of Mexico City," her uncle said. "Your grandfather was a teacher. He taught in a high school in Los Angeles for many years."

"What did they look like?" Maribel asked.

"I can show you," her aunt said. She went into the bedroom and came back with a large photo album. She sat with Maribel and went through page after page of family photos. Maribel saw her great-grandparents, grandparents, and cousins. By the end of the weekend, Maribel proudly knew the history of her family.

❥ What does Maribel want to find out?

❥ Why does Maribel ask her aunt and uncle questions instead of playing?

Name: _____ Date: _____

The Photo Album

9	Maribel wanted to know about her family history. She
19	knew her family originally came from Mexico. But she was
29	not sure exactly where they had lived. Everyone seemed to
40	be too busy to answer her questions. Some who did listen
45	just said they didn't know.
58	On a weekend trip to see her aunt and uncle, there was a
68	thunderstorm. It was too rainy to go outside, so Maribel
79	decided to ask her aunt and uncle about her family history.
86	"Your great-grandmother and great-grandfather came
97	from a little town outside of Mexico City," her uncle said.
108	"Your grandfather was a teacher. He taught in a high school
114	in Los Angeles for many years."
121	"What did they look like?" Maribel asked.
132	"I can show you," her aunt said. She went into the
143	bedroom and came back with a large photo album. She sat
153	with Maribel and went through page after page of family
160	photos. Maribel saw her great-grandparents, grandparents,
170	and cousins. By the end of the weekend, Maribel proudly
176	knew the history of her family.

✔ What does Maribel want to find out?

✔ Why does Maribel ask her aunt and uncle questions instead of playing?

Words Read	–	Errors	=	WCPM

☐ **Fall (94 WCPM)**
☐ **Winter (112 WCPM)**
☐ **Spring (123 WCPM)**

WCPM	/	Words Read	=	Accuracy %

PROSODY				
	L1	L2	L3	L4
Reading in Phrases	O	O	O	O
Pace	O	O	O	O
Syntax	O	O	O	O
Self-correction	O	O	O	O
Intonation	O	O	O	O

Chinese New Year

The Chinese New Year begins with the first new moon in the year. It ends 15 days later when the moon is full. The date of the New Year changes every year. This is because the Chinese add an extra month every few years to their calendar.

The New Year is also known as the Spring Festival. In China, this festival is an important holiday. During a traditional New Year celebration, almost all business stops. People focus on their homes and family. Houses are cleaned and food prepared to honor ancestors.

Throughout the 15 days, many feasts are held. On the first night, one fish is left and not eaten. This fish is a symbol of abundance. People eat long noodles in the first five days as a symbol of long life. The Lantern Festival is held on the last night. Children carry lanterns through the streets. For the feast on that night, round dumplings are served. They are a symbol of the full moon and the family.

☝ Why does the date of the Chinese New Year change?

☝ What is another name for the Chinese New Year?

Name: _____   Date: _____

Chinese New Year

10	The Chinese New Year begins with the first new moon
23	in the year. It ends 15 days later when the moon is full.
34	The date of the New Year changes every year. This is
44	because the Chinese add an extra month every few years
47	to their calendar.
58	The New Year is also known as the Spring Festival. In
67	China, this festival is an important holiday. During a
75	traditional New Year celebration, almost all business stops.
85	People focus on their homes and family. Houses are cleaned
91	and food prepared to honor ancestors.
101	Throughout the 15 days, many feasts are held. On the
114	first night, one fish is left and not eaten. This fish is a
124	symbol of abundance. People eat long noodles in the first
136	five days as a symbol of long life. The Lantern Festival is
146	held on the last night. Children carry lanterns through the
156	streets. For the feast on that night, round dumplings are
168	served. They are a symbol of the full moon and the family.

✔ Why does the date of the Chinese New Year change?

✔ What is another name for the Chinese New Year?

Words Read	–	Errors	=	WCPM

☐ **Fall (94 WCPM)**
☐ **Winter (112 WCPM)**
☐ **Spring (123 WCPM)**

WCPM	/	Words Read	=	Accuracy %

PROSODY				
	L1	L2	L3	L4
Reading in Phrases	O	O	O	O
Pace	O	O	O	O
Syntax	O	O	O	O
Self-correction	O	O	O	O
Intonation	O	O	O	O

Toothbrush Trivia

The toothbrush, like the one you use everyday, has been in use for only about 75 years. The modern toothbrush has nylon bristles. It was invented in 1938. So how did people clean their teeth before that time?

Amazingly, ancient forms of toothbrushes have been found that are over five thousand years old! They are thin twigs with one end chewed. The chewing made the end into a brush. The stick was then rubbed against the teeth to clean them.

In the late 1400s, the Chinese invented a toothbrush that used bristles. The bristles were made from hog hair. The rough hairs came from the back of a hog's neck. They were put on a handle made of bone or bamboo.

Before World War II, people did not take care of their teeth like we do today. Soldiers in the war were given toothbrushes. These were modern brushes with nylon bristles. The soldiers were told to brush their teeth. People heard what the soldiers did. So they began to use toothbrushes on their own teeth.

👆 How old are the earliest toothbrushes?

👆 What caused more people to use toothbrushes in the twentieth century?

Name: _____ Date: _____

Toothbrush Trivia

10	The toothbrush, like the one you use everyday, has been
21	in use for only about 75 years. The modern toothbrush has
32	nylon bristles. It was invented in 1938. So how did people
38	clean their teeth before that time?
45	Amazingly, ancient forms of toothbrushes have been
56	found that are over five thousand years old! They are thin
66	twigs with one end chewed. The chewing made the end
78	into a brush. The stick was then rubbed against the teeth to
80	clean them.
90	In the late 1400s, the Chinese invented a toothbrush that
100	used bristles. The bristles were made from hog hair. The
112	rough hairs came from the back of a hog's neck. They were
121	put on a handle made of bone or bamboo.
132	Before World War II, people did not take care of their
143	teeth like we do today. Soldiers in the war were given
150	toothbrushes. These were modern brushes with nylon
160	bristles. The soldiers were told to brush their teeth. People
170	heard what the soldiers did. So they began to use
175	toothbrushes on their own teeth.

✓ How old are the earliest toothbrushes?

✓ What caused more people to use toothbrushes in the twentieth century?

Words Read	–	Errors	=	WCPM

☐ **Fall (94 WCPM)**
☐ **Winter (112 WCPM)**
☐ **Spring (123 WCPM)**

WCPM	/	Words Read	=	Accuracy %

PROSODY				
	L1	L2	L3	L4
Reading in Phrases	O	O	O	O
Pace	O	O	O	O
Syntax	O	O	O	O
Self-correction	O	O	O	O
Intonation	O	O	O	O

Fireball

Rico loved stargazing. He spent a few hours every clear night watching the skies. His sister thought he was wasting time, but Rico knew he wasn't. As he patiently watched, he saw amazing sights. He had seen the streak of a comet's tail and watched a space station whiz by.

Rico's favorite nights for watching the skies were when there was a meteor shower. These happened about four times a year. On one August night, he planned to see the Perseid shower, so he invited his sister to watch too.

"How boring!" his sister said. "You just sit and watch the sky?"

"Just try it," Rico said. At last, he convinced her to watch the sky with him.

After an hour, Rico's sister was bored and grumbling. She threatened to leave when suddenly a bright flash appeared and a fireball zipped across the sky. Rico and his sister could hear it crackle and sizzle as it burned. Then it disappeared over the horizon. Rico's sister was amazed. She would never again think that watching the sky was boring.

☞ What does Rico like to do?

☞ How does Rico's sister change at the end of the passage?

Name: _____ Date: _____

Fireball

10	Rico loved stargazing. He spent a few hours every clear
20	night watching the skies. His sister thought he was wasting
31	time, but Rico knew he wasn't. As he patiently watched, he
43	saw amazing sights. He had seen the streak of a comet's tail
50	and watched a space station whiz by.
59	Rico's favorite nights for watching the skies were when
68	there was a meteor shower. These happened about four
80	times a year. On one August night, he planned to see the
90	Perseid shower, so he invited his sister to watch too.
100	"How boring!" his sister said. "You just sit and watch
102	the sky?"
114	"Just try it," Rico said. At last, he convinced her to watch
118	the sky with him.
128	After an hour, Rico's sister was bored and grumbling. She
137	threatened to leave when suddenly a bright flash appeared
149	and a fireball zipped across the sky. Rico and his sister could
160	hear it crackle and sizzle as it burned. Then it disappeared
170	over the horizon. Rico's sister was amazed. She would never
178	again think that watching the sky was boring.

✓ What does Rico like to do?

✓ How does Rico's sister change at the end of the passage?

Words Read	–	Errors	=	WCPM

☐ **Fall (94 WCPM)**
☐ **Winter (112 WCPM)**
☐ **Spring (123 WCPM)**

WCPM	/	Words Read	=	Accuracy %

PROSODY				
	L1	L2	L3	L4
Reading in Phrases	O	O	O	O
Pace	O	O	O	O
Syntax	O	O	O	O
Self-correction	O	O	O	O
Intonation	O	O	O	O

Just One Rule

Long ago, there was a small village that had been established by people who did not like to be told what to do. So their village had no rules or regulations.

Everything was fine for a while. Then arguments began to break out. One woman complained that her neighbor did not get rid of his garbage fast enough. Another woman accused her neighbor of playing loud music late at night. Someone else announced that the big plastic flamingo he had put in his front yard had been stolen.

Finally, the people had a meeting. Everyone talked and shouted at once. At last, one man asked for quiet and said, "Someone has to conduct this meeting or we won't get anything done. It might as well be me." They all agreed and were quiet.

The man said, "I propose just one rule. Don't do anything to anyone else that you wouldn't want done to you. If you have a problem, then have a talk with me. But remember that I am not in charge." So everyone was happy after "Not in Charge" took charge.

✔ Why did the village have no rules?

✔ Why does the one rule make everyone happy?

Name: _____   Date: _____

Just One Rule

10	Long ago, there was a small village that had been
22	established by people who did not like to be told what to
31	do. So their village had no rules or regulations.
40	Everything was fine for a while. Then arguments began
50	to break out. One woman complained that her neighbor did
60	not get rid of his garbage fast enough. Another woman
70	accused her neighbor of playing loud music late at night.
79	Someone else announced that the big plastic flamingo he
88	had put in his front yard had been stolen.
97	Finally, the people had a meeting. Everyone talked and
109	shouted at once. At last, one man asked for quiet and said,
119	"Someone has to conduct this meeting or we won't get
131	anything done. It might as well be me." They all agreed and
133	were quiet.
144	The man said, "I propose just one rule. Don't do anything
156	to anyone else that you wouldn't want done to you. If you
167	have a problem, then have a talk with me. But remember
178	that I am not in charge." So everyone was happy after
183	"Not in Charge" took charge.

✔ Why did the village have no rules?

✔ Why does the one rule make everyone happy?

Words Read	–	Errors	=	WCPM

☐ **Fall (94 WCPM)**
☐ **Winter (112 WCPM)**
☐ **Spring (123 WCPM)**

WCPM	/	Words Read	=	Accuracy %

PROSODY				
	L1	L2	L3	L4
Reading in Phrases	O	O	O	O
Pace	O	O	O	O
Syntax	O	O	O	O
Self-correction	O	O	O	O
Intonation	O	O	O	O

Too Many Cats

Mr. Bixby had two big orange cats that he was very proud of. One had a magnificent long and bushy tail. The other cat was beautiful, with fur the color of marmalade jam.

The cats in the town knew that Mr. Bixby loved cats. So they were careful not to bother the birds around his home. They did not meow around his open window late at night.

One day, there was a big storm with several inches of rain. Many parts of the town were flooded. Mr. Bixby was fortunate that his house was on a hill, so his home was high and dry.

The day after the storm, Mr. Bixby went down into his basement. He was startled to find that the basement was full of many cats. "There are too many cats in here," he cried. "Where did they all come from?"

Mr. Bixby finally figured out why the cats were in the basement. They came to get away from the flood. So he began to call all of the townspeople. Everyone was thrilled their cats had been found safe and sound.

👆 How are Mr. Bixby's cats alike?

👆 Where do the cats go to escape the flood?

Name: _____ Date: _____

Too Many Cats

11	Mr. Bixby had two big orange cats that he was very
21	proud of. One had a magnificent long and bushy tail.
31	The other cat was beautiful, with fur the color of
33	marmalade jam.
45	The cats in the town knew that Mr. Bixby loved cats. So
56	they were careful not to bother the birds around his home.
67	They did not meow around his open window late at night.
78	One day, there was a big storm with several inches of
89	rain. Many parts of the town were flooded. Mr. Bixby was
102	fortunate that his house was on a hill, so his home was high
104	and dry.
115	The day after the storm, Mr. Bixby went down into his
126	basement. He was startled to find that the basement was full
138	of many cats. "There are too many cats in here," he cried.
144	"Where did they all come from?"
155	Mr. Bixby finally figured out why the cats were in the
166	basement. They came to get away from the flood. So he
176	began to call all of the townspeople. Everyone was thrilled
184	their cats had been found safe and sound.

✓ How are Mr. Bixby's cats alike?

✓ Where do the cats go to escape the flood?

Words Read	–	Errors	=	WCPM

☐ **Fall (94 WCPM)**
☐ **Winter (112 WCPM)**
☐ **Spring (123 WCPM)**

WCPM	/	Words Read	=	Accuracy %

PROSODY				
	L1	L2	L3	L4
Reading in Phrases	O	O	O	O
Pace	O	O	O	O
Syntax	O	O	O	O
Self-correction	O	O	O	O
Intonation	O	O	O	O

Scoring Sheets and Answer Keys

Name: _____ Date: _____

WEEKLY ASSESSMENT SCORING SHEET   UNIT ___ WEEK ___

Item	Content Focus/CCSS	Score	Comments
1			
2			
3			
4			
5			

Assessment · Scoring Sheet

Name: _____ Date: _____

MID-UNIT SCORING SHEET   UNIT __

Item	Content Focus/CCSS	Score	Comments
1			
2			
3			
4			
5			
6			
7			
8			
9			
10			

Name: _____ Date: _____

UNIT ASSESSMENT SCORING SHEET   UNIT __

Item	Content Focus/CCSS	Score	Comments
1			
2			
3			
4			
5			
6			
7			
8			
9			
10			
11			
12			
13			
14			
15			

Name: _____ Date: _____

EXIT ASSESSMENT SCORING SHEET   UNIT __

Item	Content Focus/CCSS	Score	Comments
1			
2			
3			
4			
5			
6			
7			
8			
9			
10			
11			
12			
13			
14			
15			

Weekly Assessment Answer Key

UNIT 1 WEEK 1

Item #	Content Focus	CCSS
1	Vocabulary: Context Clues	L.4.4a
2	Sequence	RL.4.3
3	Vocabulary: Context Clues	L.4.4a
4	Sequence	RL.4.3
5	Sequence	RL.4.3

Suggested Responses:

1 **Text Evidence:** wildly

2 She tries to find her way home.

3 to think about something
Text Evidence: "I must think about a way to get to the other side," she said.

4 **Text Evidence:** Soon, she heard loud footsteps.

5 **Text Evidence:** Then, he stretched his fingertips to one side and his toes to the other. Then

UNIT 1 WEEK 2

Item #	Content Focus	CCSS
1	Problem and Solution	RL.4.1
2	Vocabulary: Context Clues	L.4.4a
3	Problem and Solution	RL.4.1
4	Vocabulary: Context Clues	L.4.4a
5	Problem and Solution	RL.4.1

Suggested Responses:

1 **Text Evidence:** "I'd like to play on the team, but I'm not good enough."

2 **Text Evidence:** for a few seconds
paused or stopped for a moment

3 Becky helps Kim practice her soccer skills.
Text Evidence: First, she helped Kim practice moving the ball with her feet.

4 **Text Evidence:** believe in yourself

5 Kim joins the soccer team and scores a winning goal.
Text Evidence: "I feel pretty good about my soccer skills now!"

UNIT 1 WEEK 3

Item #	Content Focus	CCSS
1	Compare and Contrast	RI.4.5
2	Vocabulary: Context Clues	L.4.4a
3	Compare and Contrast	RI.4.5
4	Vocabulary: Context Clues	L.4.4a
5	Compare and Contrast	RI.4.5

Suggested Responses:

1 **Text Evidence:** Hurricanes and earthquakes are natural disasters. They can quickly change the surface of Earth. Some changes are similar for both hurricanes and earthquakes.

2 **Text Evidence:** The winds can tear up trees and buildings. The floods can destroy beaches and roads.
the act of breaking apart or ruining

3 Possible answers: Hurricanes start over oceans, and earthquakes start inside Earth. Hurricanes have strong winds and flooding, and earthquakes shake Earth.
Text Evidence: Unlike

4 **Text Evidence:** crumble
break down or fall apart

5 **Text Evidence:** underground; makes the ground shake

UNIT 1 WEEK 4

Item #	Content Focus	CCSS
1	Cause and Effect	RI.4.3
2	Cause and Effect	RI.4.3
3	Vocabulary: Context Clues	L.4.4a
4	Cause and Effect	RI.4.3
5	Vocabulary: Context Clues	L.4.4a

Suggested Responses:

1 to learn about musical instruments
Text Evidence: "You can learn about some instruments there."

2 **Text Evidence:** Sound is made

3 **Text Evidence:** exciting

4 You make a buzzing sound into the mouthpiece.
Text Evidence: He pointed to the mouthpiece. "You put your lips here and buzz," he said.

5 **Text Evidence:** skills

UNIT 1 WEEK 5

Item #	Content Focus	CCSS
1	Vocabulary: Context Clues	L.4.4a
2	Main Idea and Key Details	RI.4.2
3	Main Idea and Key Details	RI.4.2
4	Main Idea and Key Details	RI.4.2
5	Vocabulary: Context Clues	L.4.4a

Suggested Responses:

1 **Text Evidence:** a new kind of organization; run by kids
It is made up of kids who help kids. This is a new and original idea.

2 Kids Helping Kids is a new and different kind of organization.

3 **Text Evidence:** How Does It Work?
kids of all different backgrounds

4 **Text Evidence:** what they like to do; how to lead others; the importance of helping others

5 **Text Evidence:** It wants to help kids around the world get clean water.
activity or plan

UNIT 2 WEEK 1

Item #	Content Focus	CCSS
1	Vocabulary: Context Clues	L.4.4a
2	Theme	RL.4.2
3	Vocabulary: Context Clues	L.4.4a
4	Theme	RL.4.2
5	Theme	RL.4.2

Suggested Responses:

1 **Text Evidence:** truthful

2 He wants her to take him to the fruit.

3 **Text Evidence:** He jumped on the plums and ate all of them; He jumped on the bananas and ate them, too; He did not share anything!
not sharing with others; wanting more than you need

4 **Text Evidence:** Next, the girl took the spider to a tree and pointed to a small hole.
She wants to teach the spider a lesson about taking too much for himself.

5 **Text Evidence:** When he tried to come out, he was stuck. He had eaten so much that he could not fit through the hole.
He should only take what he needs and nothing more.

UNIT 2 WEEK 2

Item #	Content Focus	CCSS
1	Vocabulary: Context Clues	L.4.4a
2	Theme	RL.4.2
3	Vocabulary: Context Clues	L.4.4a
4	Theme	RL.4.2
5	Theme	RL.4.2

Suggested Responses:

1 **Text Evidence:** *in a bad mood; Angrily*
grumpy or angry

2 Raccoon keeps waking up Squirrel at night when he looks for food.

3 **Text Evidence:** *knocks over a trashcan; bang the lids*
something that causes a lot of noise

4 Squirrel collects food for Raccoon during the day.
Text Evidence: You can eat it at night instead of looking through trashcans.
Then we will both be happy.

5 They learn that they can solve their problems if they work together.

UNIT 2 WEEK 3

Item #	Content Focus	CCSS
1	Vocabulary: Context Clues	L.4.4a
2	Main Idea and Key Details	RI.4.2
3	Vocabulary: Context Clues	L.4.4a
4	Main Idea and Key Details	RI.4.2
5	Main Idea and Key Details	RI.4.2

Suggested Responses:

1 **Text Evidence:** dinosaurs
still exist

2 all around the world

3 **Text Evidence:** done well

4 **Text Evidence:** They fly from plant to plant. They sip nectar from flowers.
Butterflies are active during the day.

5 Butterflies sip nectar from flowers. Lizards eat butterflies.
Text Evidence: Butterflies are part of a food chain.

UNIT 2 WEEK 4

Item #	Content Focus	CCSS
1	Main Idea and Key Details	RI.4.2
2	Vocabulary: Context Clues	L.4.4a
3	Main Idea and Key Details	RI.4.2
4	Vocabulary: Context Clues	L.4.4a
5	Main Idea and Key Details	RI.4.2

Suggested Responses:

1. **Text Evidence:** Zebras, tigers, and some fish

2. **Text Evidence:** The color or shape of the animals helps them look like part of their surroundings. This makes them hard to see.
hidden or disguised

3. **Text Evidence:** Body color helps some animals blend in with their surroundings; Other animals have special patterns or markings; Some animals blend in because they look like other things.

4. **Text Evidence:** who hunt the animals for food
one that hunts another for food

5. Animals use different kinds of camouflage to help them stay safe.

UNIT 2 WEEK 5

Item #	Content Focus	CCSS
1	Genre	RL.4.5
2	Literary Elements: Rhyme	RL.4.5
3	Literary Elements: Simile	RL.5.4
4	Point of View	RL.4.6
5	Point of View	RL.4.6

Suggested Responses:

1. It has meter and rhyme. It also shows some of the speaker's feelings.

2. **Text Evidence:** little/brittle; mine/vine

3. **Text Evidence:** like a clown
a monkey and a clown

4. No. The speaker does not use "I" or "me" to describe the events in the poem.

5. The speaker feels bad for the tiger.
Text Evidence: Poor Tiger

UNIT 3 WEEK 1

Item #	Content Focus	CCSS
1	Vocabulary: Context Clues	L.4.4a
2	Point of View	RL.4.6
3	Vocabulary: Context Clues	L.4.4a
4	Point of View	RL.4.6
5	Point of View	RL.4.6

Suggested Responses:

1. **Text Evidence:** different items; a mess of things
   a mixture or an assortment

2. third-person point of view
   Text Evidence: she, her

3. **Text Evidence:** in case there is something sharp inside
   It means to do it carefully.

4. Padma thinks it is strange to play with a girl from a picture frame, but she does not want to hurt the girl's feelings.

5. **Text Evidence:** Padma grinned and thought, "This is amazing!"

UNIT 3 WEEK 2

Item #	Content Focus	CCSS
1	Point of View	RL.4.6
2	Vocabulary: Context Clues	L.4.4a
3	Point of View	RL.4.6
4	Vocabulary: Context Clues	L.4.4a
5	Point of View	RL.4.6

Suggested Responses:

1. It is told in the first-person point of view.
   Text Evidence: I

2. **Text Evidence:** the task of making posters
   gave a task to be done

3. Possible answer: Max wants to help out by joining a community service project.

4. **Text Evidence:** "The people who live in our town"

5. Max feels good about the project and knows it will be a success.
   Text Evidence: It felt good to be helping the community. We knew our project would be a success, and we'd be helping planet Earth, too!

UNIT 3 WEEK 3

Item #	Content Focus	CCSS
1	Vocabulary: Context Clues	L.4.4a
2	Author's Point of View	RI.4.8
3	Vocabulary: Context Clues	L.4.4a
4	Author's Point of View	RI.4.8
5	Author's Point of View	RI.4.8

Suggested Responses:

1 **Text Evidence:** able to do the job
O'Connor graduated law school and was able to do the job of a lawyer.

2 **Text Evidence:** did something wonderful

3 **Text Evidence:** hope
Possible answer: She showed that women can do great things just like men can.

4 The author probably believes that everyone deserves the same rights.
Text Evidence: She tried to protect the rights of Americans. She helped to create laws that were fair for everyone.

5 **Text Evidence:** O'Connor becomes the first female judge in the U.S. Supreme Court; O'Connor is given the Presidential Medal of Freedom.

UNIT 3 WEEK 4

Item #	Content Focus	CCSS
1	Author's Point of View	RI.4.8
2	Vocabulary: Context Clues	L.4.4a
3	Author's Point of View	RI.4.8
4	Vocabulary: Context Clues	L.4.4a
5	Author's Point of View	RI.4.8

Suggested Responses:

1 The author thinks it is amazing.

2 **Text Evidence:** In his speech
a speech to a group of people

3 **Text Evidence:** "Ask not what your country can do for you, but what you can do for your country."
Possible answer: His words led young people to make a difference in the world and help others.

4 **Text Evidence:** broken

5 The author admires Kennedy as a leader for inspiring so many people.
Text Evidence: . . . he worked hard to improve people's lives. His words led many others to do the same.

Weekly Assessment • Answer Key

UNIT 3 WEEK 5

Item #	Content Focus	CCSS
1	Author's Point of View	RI.4.8
2	Vocabulary: Context Clues	L.4.4a
3	Author's Point of View	RI.4.8
4	Vocabulary: Context Clues	L.4.4a
5	Author's Point of View	RI.4.8

Suggested Responses:

1. **Text Evidence:** Can you imagine life without the Internet?
Possible answer: In today's world, many people use the Internet.

2. **Text Evidence:** made the Internet available to the public; made it available almost everywhere today
improvements or gains

3. **Text Evidence:** There are many good things about the Internet.

4. **Text Evidence:** dangers; cause parents to worry
reasons to worry

5. The author wants us to learn about Internet safety.

UNIT 4 WEEK 1

Item #	Content Focus	CCSS
1	Cause and Effect	RI.4.3
2	Vocabulary: Context Clues	L.4.4a
3	Cause and Effect	RI.4.3
4	Vocabulary: Context Clues	L.4.4a
5	Cause and Effect	RI.4.3

Suggested Responses:

1. **Text Evidence:** That is because there were no schools available.
Most children never learned how to read or write.

2. **Text Evidence:** (lej•is•LAY•shuhn)
laws

3. They had to pay a fine if they did not obey the law.

4. **Text Evidence:** promise

5. The United States has a free public education system.
Text Evidence: free

UNIT 4 WEEK 2

Item #	Content Focus	CCSS
1	Point of View	RL.4.6
2	Point of View	RL.4.6
3	Vocabulary: Context Clues	L.4.4a
4	Vocabulary: Context Clues	L.4.4a
5	Point of View	RL.4.6

Suggested Responses:

1 **Text Evidence:** I; my
Eva

2 **Text Evidence:** "Unbelievable—I was just wearing jeans!" I thought to myself.
The narrator is shocked and amazed because her clothing changed on its own.

3 **Text Evidence:** no one ran against Washington

4 **Text Evidence:** give speeches or do activities to get elected
an organized plan to do something

5 **Text Evidence:** "Wow!" I said to myself. I couldn't wait to get home and tell my mother
what I just saw.

UNIT 4 WEEK 3

Item #	Content Focus	CCSS
1	Point of View	RL.4.6
2	Point of View	RL.4.6
3	Vocabulary: Context Clues	L.4.4a
4	Point of View	RL.4.6
5	Vocabulary: Context Clues	L.4.4a

Suggested Responses:

1 No; the pronouns his and he show that a third-person narrator is telling the story.

2 **Text Evidence:** "Henry Ford's Model T car is fantastic! … I can't wait to buy one someday!"

3 **Text Evidence:** by looking down Main Street and then searching the side streets
looked or searched

4 Matthew stutters when he asks Mr. Bond a question. The ellipses in the sentence show that
he pauses.
Text Evidence: "Good! I…ummm…was wondering…"

5 **Text Evidence:** just like a diamond!
sparkling or shining brightly

UNIT 4 WEEK 4

Item #	Content Focus	CCSS
1	Vocabulary: Context Clues	L.4.4a
2	Cause and Effect	RI.4.3
3	Vocabulary: Context Clues	L.4.4a
4	Cause and Effect	RI.4.3
5	Cause and Effect	RI.4.3

Suggested Responses:

1. **Text Evidence:** This is a scientist who studies the night sky.

2. It helps objects appear clear through a telescope and not fuzzy.

3. **Text Evidence:** This tube-shaped instrument helps you view distant objects.
   a tool used to view faraway objects

4. The diagram shows the different parts of a telescope.
   Text Evidence: eyepiece

5. **Text Evidence:** our planet moves in a circle around the Sun
   Astronomers are able to view the night sky when day turns to night.

UNIT 4 WEEK 5

Item #	Content Focus	CCSS
1	Literary Elements: Stanza	RL.4.5
2	Theme	RL.4.2
3	Literary Elements: Repetition	RL.4.5
4	Theme	RL.4.2
5	Genre	RL.4.5

Suggested Responses:

1. **Text Evidence:** An unsafe speedway

2. The narrator thinks that Pine Road is dangerous and wants to get across it safely.

3. **Text Evidence:** STOP!
   The poem is about getting a STOP sign put up on Pine Road so the cars will stop and make it safe to cross the street.

4. **Text Evidence:** The council members agree—the signs will go up!
   Pine Road will be safer with a STOP sign. The narrator no longer has to worry about crossing it.

5. The narrator tells how a problem with crossing Pine Road is solved.

UNIT 5 WEEK 1

Item #	Content Focus	CCSS
1	Vocabulary: Context Clues	L.4.4a
2	Problem and Solution	RL.4.1
3	Problem and Solution	RL.4.1
4	Vocabulary: Context Clues	L.4.4a
5	Problem and Solution	RL.4.1

Suggested Responses:

1 **Text Evidence:** photographs

2 Mrs. Brown is having hip surgery and will be in the hospital for a few days.

3 **Text Evidence:** One day, Mrs. Brown seemed sad.
Raj offers to have Lucky stay at his house. He will care for Lucky while Mrs. Brown is in the hospital.

4 **Text Evidence:** wagged his tail
show or communicate in some way

5 **Text Evidence:** Mrs. Brown needed to use a walker for a while to get around. She could not walk Lucky or feed him easily.
Raj says he will come to Mrs. Brown's house every day to feed and walk Lucky.

UNIT 5 WEEK 2

Item #	Content Focus	CCSS
1	Cause and Effect	RL.4.3
2	Vocabulary: Context Clues	L.4.4a
3	Cause and Effect	RL.4.3
4	Vocabulary: Context Clues	L.4.4a
5	Cause and Effect	RL.4.3

Suggested Responses:

1 **Text Evidence:** Johnny wants plant apple trees where people live out west.
so no one would be hungry

2 **Text Evidence:** homes in new lands
places where people have come to live

3 He makes friends with people and animals. He even protects insects.
Text Evidence: Once he put out a campfire with his bare hands

4 **Text Evidence:** laughed

5 Johnny Appleseed
Text Evidence: He planted thousands of apple trees. He gave away seeds for people to plant their own trees.

UNIT 5 WEEK 3

Item #	Content Focus	CCSS
1	Vocabulary: Context Clues	L.4.4a
2	Problem and Solution	RI.4.5
3	Problem and Solution	RI.4.5
4	Vocabulary: Context Clues	L.4.4a
5	Problem and Solution	RI.4.5

Suggested Responses:

1 **Text Evidence:** real love for sports
real or true

2 **Text Evidence:** In the winter of 1891, it was too cold to exercise outdoors. He needed a new indoor game for his students to play
He invented basketball, a game that his students could play indoors.

3 **Text Evidence:** Each time a player scored, someone had to climb up a ladder to get the ball out of the basket.
The baskets eventually became open hoops with nets.

4 **Text Evidence:** Through the years; Eventually; still used in these times

5 **Text Evidence:** Naismith organizes the first basketball game..

UNIT 5 WEEK 4

Item #	Content Focus	CCSS
1	Sequence	RI.4.3
2	Vocabulary: Context Clues	L.4.4a
3	Sequence	RI.4.3
4	Vocabulary: Context Clues	L.4.4a
5	Sequence	RI.4.3

Suggested Responses:

1 **Text Evidence:** First, Next, After, then
The events tell how an MRI test works.

2 **Text Evidence:** making it larger
easier

3 **Text Evidence:** The first MRI test on a human was done in 1977.
Scientists have improved MRI technology since 1977. The test takes less time and produces more pictures.

4 normal

5 They decide the best way to treat their patients.

UNIT 5 WEEK 5

Item #	Content Focus	CCSS
1	Sequence	RI.4.5
2	Vocabulary: Context Clues	L.4.4a
3	Sequence	RI.4.5
4	Vocabulary: Context Clues	L.4.4a
5	Sequence	RI.4.5

Suggested Responses:

1 **Text Evidence:** 2005
around 1818

2 **Text Evidence:** Two sperm-whale teeth were found in the ship.
proof

3 **Text Evidence:** Its final trip was in 1855.
It was the last ship to be broken apart in a ship-breaking yard.

4 **Text Evidence:** trip
a voyage or trip made for a certain reason

5 **Text Evidence:** San Francisco

UNIT 6 WEEK 1

Item #	Content Focus	CCSS
1	Theme	RL.4.2
2	Vocabulary: Context Clues	L.4.4a
3	Vocabulary: Context Clues	L.4.4a
4	Theme	RL.4.2
5	Theme	RL.4.2

Suggested Responses:

1 **Text Evidence:** "It is time to make *burekas*, so please prepare the crust and filling."
"It's a tradition. Our family has always made burekas . . ."
to remember what is important to their family

2 **Text Evidence:** "your ancestors—my grandparents—made them"
members of the same family who lived long ago, before you

3 **Text Evidence:** Our family shows respect by keeping this tradition.
a source of respect

4 **Text Evidence:** Sarah wanted to treat her brothers to the moving picture show. It could be their monthly tradition.

5 She is proud and happy.
Text Evidence: Mother hugged Sarah. "You are a good girl, Sarah. That will be a nice tradition to start."

UNIT 6 WEEK 2

Item #	Content Focus	CCSS
1	Vocabulary: Context Clues	L.4.4a
2	Theme	RL.4.2
3	Vocabulary: Context Clues	L.4.4a
4	Theme	RL.4.2
5	Theme	RL.4.2

Suggested Responses:

1 **Text Evidence:** describes

2 **Text Evidence:** *Thank goodness, my family passed the test, and we did not have to return to Italy!*

3 **Text Evidence:** The doctor lifted up our eyelids; awful exam
strongly disliked

4 **Text Evidence:** *Uncle Carlo waited for us in this room. We ran to him, kissed, and sighed with relief because we were now in America.*
Families kissed their loved ones here when they came to America.

5 A time capsule can include people's writings, drawings, or belongings that show what life was like in the past.

UNIT 6 WEEK 3

Item #	Content Focus	CCSS
1	Main Idea and Key Details	RI.4.2
2	Vocabulary: Context Clues	L.4.4a
3	Main Idea and Key Details	RI.4.2
4	Vocabulary: Context Clues	L.4.4a
5	Main Idea and Key Details	RI.4.2

Suggested Responses:

1 **Text Evidence:** Think about sitting in a dark cave, huddled under an animal hide— shivering through the night!

2 **Text Evidence:** that never ran out
able to be used again and again

3 They may have seen fire when lightning struck a tree. They might have felt how warm it was and carried a burning branch back to the cave.

4 **Text Evidence:** changed

5 The discovery of fire as an energy source improved people's lives and helped them to survive.
Text Evidence: From there, people built their own fires and discovered that fire cooked food and helped them make tools for hunting. How life-changing fire must have been! It helped many people survive long ago.

UNIT 6 WEEK 4

Item #	Content Focus	CCSS
1	Vocabulary: Context Clues	L.4.4a
2	Vocabulary: Context Clues	L.4.4a
3	Main Idea and Key Details	RI.4.2
4	Main Idea and Key Details	RI.4.2
5	Main Idea and Key Details	RI.4.2

Suggested Responses:

1. **Text Evidence:** Each time you give money to buy something, a transaction takes place. the act of buying or selling something

2. **Text Evidence:** Paper bills
money

3. **Text Evidence:** Each bill has a design and code that identify it.

4. It prints the background colors and images onto the paper and helps to make the final finished image on the money.

5. **Text Evidence:** [Students should draw a box around the section titled, "From the Printing Press to You."]
After money in printed, it goes to banks.

UNIT 6 WEEK 5

Item #	Content Focus	CCSS
1	Theme	RL.4.2
2	Literary Elements: Imagery	RL.4.5
3	Literary Elements: Personification	RL.4.5
4	Theme	RL.4.2
5	Genre	RL.4.5

Suggested Responses:

1. **Text Evidence:** Mom says "Slow down!" when we gobble dinner— / We are both "lefties," / We both have a silly sense of humor

2. They look the same because they wear the same things and act the same way.
Text Evidence: On Sundays, we have a tradition of watching football. We pop the popcorn, slip on our blue jerseys, sit on the couch, our left ankle crossed over right.

3. **Text Evidence:** roots growing deep and wide—introducing me to new people, places, and things.

4. **Text Evidence:** I can play sports well, while he has two left feet. / My voice is sharp and high-pitched: / His is deep, gentle, and low.
He wonders if he will change as he grows older, but he is also happy about who he is.

5. The poem does not rhyme.

Mid-Unit Assessment Answer Key

UNIT 1

Item #	Answer	Content Focus	CCSS
1	B	Vocabulary: Context Clues	L.4.4a
2	C	Sequence	RL.4.3
3	C	Problem and Solution	RL.4.1
4	A	Problem and Solution	RL.4.1
5	A	Sequence	RL.4.3
6	B	Compare and Contrast	RI.4.5
7	A	Vocabulary: Context Clues	L.4.4a
8	A	Compare and Contrast	RI.4.5
9	C	Vocabulary: Context Clues	L.4.4a
10	C	Text Features: Diagram	RI.4.7

UNIT 2

Item #	Answer	Content Focus	CCSS
1	C	Vocabulary: Context Clues	L.4.4a
2	A	Theme	RL.4.2
3	B	Vocabulary: Context Clues	L.4.4a
4	C	Theme	RL.4.2
5	A	Theme	RL.4.2
6	C	Vocabulary: Context Clues	L.4.4a
7	A	Main Idea and Details	RI.4.2
8	A	Main Idea and Details	RI.4.2
9	B	Text Features: Flow Chart	RI.4.7
10	B	Main Idea and Details	RI.4.2

Mid-Unit Assessment • Answer Key

UNIT 3

Item #	Answer	Content Focus	CCSS
1	A	Point of View	RL.4.6
2	C	Point of View	RL.4.6
3	B	Vocabulary: Context Clues	L.4.4a
4	C	Vocabulary: Context Clues	L.4.4a
5	B	Point of View	RL.4.6
6	A	Author's Point of View	RI.4.8
7	B	Author's Point of View	RI.4.8
8	C	Vocabulary: Context Clues	L.4.4a
9	A	Author's Point of View	RI.4.8
10	B	Text Features: Time Line	RI.4.7

Item #	Answer	Content Focus	CCSS
1	B	Point of View	RL.4.6
2	A	Vocabulary: Context Clues	L.4.4a
3	C	Point of View	RL.4.6
4	B	Vocabulary: Context Clues	L.4.4a
5	C	Point of View	RL.4.6
6	B	Cause and Effect	RI.4.3
7	A	Text Features: Pronunciation	RI.4.7
8	A	Cause and Effect	RI.4.3
9	C	Vocabulary: Context Clues	L.4.4a
10	C	Cause and Effect	RI.4.3

UNIT 5

Item #	Answer	Content Focus	CCSS
1	A	Problem and Solution	RL.4.1
2	B	Problem and Solution	RL.4.1
3	B	Cause and Effect	RL.4.3
4	A	Vocabulary: Context Clues	L.4.4a
5	B	Cause and Effect	RL.4.3
6	C	Problem and Solution	RI.4.5
7	C	Problem and Solution	RI.4.5
8	A	Vocabulary: Context Clues	L.4.4a
9	B	Vocabulary: Context Clues	L.4.4a
10	B	Text Features: Time Line	RI.4.7

UNIT 6

Item #	Answer	Content Focus	CCSS
1	A	Vocabulary: Context Clues	L.4.4a
2	C	Vocabulary: Context Clues	L.4.4a
3	A	Theme	RL.4.2
4	C	Theme	RL.4.2
5	B	Theme	RL.4.2
6	A	Vocabulary: Context Clues	L.4.4a
7	B	Main Idea and Key Details	RI.4.2
8	B	Main Idea and Key Details	RI.4.2
9	A	Main Idea and Key Details	RI.4.2
10	C	Main Idea and Key Details	RI.4.2

Unit Assessment Answer Key

UNIT 1

Item #	Answer	Content Focus	CCSS
1	C	Problem and Solution	RL.4.1
2	C	Vocabulary: Context Clues	L.4.4a
3	A	Vocabulary: Context Clues	L.4.4a
4	C	Problem and Solution	RL.4.1
5	A	Sequence	RL.4.3
6	B	Vocabulary: Context Clues	L.4.4a
7	B	Sequence	RL.4.3
8	A	Vocabulary: Context Clues	L.4.4a
9	B	Vocabulary: Context Clues	L.4.4a
10	A	Compare and Contrast	RI.4.5
11	C	Cause and Effect	RI.4.3
12	C	Cause and Effect	RI.4.3
13	A	Main Idea and Key Details	RI.4.2
14	C	Text Features: Chart	RI.4.7
15	B	Compare and Contrast	RI.4.5

UNIT 2

Item #	Answer	Content Focus	CCSS
1	B	Point of View	RL.4.6
2	A	Theme	RL.4.2
3	B	Point of View	RL.4.6
4	C	Vocabulary: Context Clues	L.4.4a
5	C	Vocabulary: Context Clues	L.4.4a
6	A	Theme	RL.4.2
7	B	Theme	RL.4.2
8	A	Vocabulary: Context Clues	L.4.4a
9	B	Vocabulary: Context Clues	L.4.4a
10	C	Main Idea and Details	RI.4.2
11	A	Main Idea and Details	RI.4.2
12	B	Main Idea and Details	RI.4.2
13	B	Main Idea and Details	RI.4.2
14	A	Vocabulary: Context Clues	L.4.4a
15	C	Text Features: Flow Chart	RI.4.7

UNIT 3

Item #	Answer	Content Focus	CCSS
1	C	Point of View	RL.4.6
2	C	Vocabulary: Context Clues	L.4.4a
3	A	Point of View	RL.4.6
4	B	Point of View	RL.4.6
5	B	Vocabulary: Context Clues	L.4.4a
6	C	Vocabulary: Context Clues	L.4.4a
7	A	Point of View	RL.4.6
8	A	Point of View	RL.4.6
9	B	Author's Point of View	RI.4.8
10	B	Vocabulary: Context Clues	L.4.4a
11	C	Vocabulary: Context Clues	L.4.4a
12	B	Author's Point of View	RI.4.8
13	A	Author's Point of View	RI.4.8
14	A	Author's Point of View	RI.4.8
15	B	Text Features: Time Line	RI.4.7

UNIT 4

Item #	Answer	Content Focus	CCSS
1	C	Point of View	RL.4.6
2	B	Vocabulary: Context Clues	L.4.4a
3	A	Vocabulary: Context Clues	L.4.4a
4	C	Point of View	RL.4.6
5	B	Theme	RL.4.2
6	C	Theme	RL.4.2
7	C	Point of View	RL.4.6
8	A	Vocabulary: Context Clues	L.4.4a
9	A	Vocabulary: Context Clues	L.4.4a
10	C	Cause and Effect	RI.4.3
11	B	Vocabulary: Context Clues	L.4.4a
12	C	Cause and Effect	RI.4.3
13	C	Cause and Effect	RI.4.3
14	B	Cause and Effect	RI.4.3
15	A	Text Features: Diagram	RI.4.7

312 Grade 4

Unit Assessment • Answer Key

UNIT 5

Item #	Answer	Content Focus	CCSS
1	A	Cause and Effect	RL.4.3
2	C	Vocabulary: Context Clues	L.4.4a
3	C	Problem and Solution	RL.4.1
4	B	Cause and Effect	RL.4.3
5	B	Vocabulary: Context Clues	L.4.4a
6	A	Vocabulary: Context Clues	L.4.4a
7	C	Problem and Solution	RL.4.1
8	A	Vocabulary: Context Clues	L.4.4a
9	B	Problem and Solution	RI.4.5
10	A	Sequence	RI.4.3
11	B	Vocabulary: Context Clues	L.4.4a
12	C	Sequence	RI.4.3
13	B	Sequence	RI.4.3
14	C	Problem and Solution	RI.4.5
15	C	Text Features: Map	RI.4.7

UNIT 6

Item #	Answer	Content Focus	CCSS
1	B	Vocabulary: Context Clues	L.4.4a
2	C	Theme	RL.4.2
3	C	Vocabulary: Context Clues	L.4.4a
4	A	Theme	RL.4.2
5	B	Theme	RL.4.2
6	A	Theme	RL.4.2
7	B	Theme	RL.4.2
8	B	Vocabulary: Context Clues	L.4.4a
9	A	Vocabulary: Context Clues	L.4.4a
10	C	Main Idea and Key Details	RI.4.2
11	A	Main Idea and Key Details	RI.4.2
12	B	Vocabulary: Context Clues	L.4.4a
13	C	Main Idea and Key Details	RI.4.2
14	C	Main Idea and Key Details	RI.4.2
15	A	Text Features: Glossary	RI.4.7

Unit Assessment · Answer Key

Exit Assessment Answer Key

UNIT 1

Item #	Answer	Content Focus	CCSS
1	B	Problem and Solution	RL.4.1
2	A	Sequence	RL.4.3
3	B	Vocabulary: Context Clues	L.4.4a
4	B	Vocabulary: Context Clues	L.4.4a
5	C	Problem and Solution	RL.4.1
6	A	Vocabulary: Context Clues	L.4.4a
7	A	Sequence	RL.4.3
8	B	Compare and Contrast	RI.4.5
9	A	Vocabulary: Context Clues	L.4.4a
10	C	Vocabulary: Context Clues	L.4.4a
11	B	Cause and Effect	RI.4.3
12	A	Cause and Effect	RI.4.3
13	C	Main Idea and Key Details	RI.4.2
14	A	Compare and Contrast	RI.4.5
15	A	Text Features: Chart	RI.4.7

UNIT 2

Item #	Answer	Content Focus	CCSS
1	A	Theme	RL.4.2
2	C	Point of View	RL.4.6
3	A	Point of View	RL.4.6
4	A	Vocabulary: Context Clues	L.4.4a
5	B	Vocabulary: Context Clues	L.4.4a
6	C	Point of View	RL.4.6
7	C	Theme	RL.4.2
8	A	Main Idea and Key Details	RI.4.2
9	B	Vocabulary: Context Clues	L.4.4a
10	C	Main Idea and Key Details	RI.4.2
11	C	Main Idea and Key Details	RI.4.2
12	A	Vocabulary: Context Clues	L.4.4a
13	B	Vocabulary: Context Clues	L.4.4a
14	C	Main Idea and Key Details	RI.4.2
15	B	Text Features: Flow Chart	RI.4.7

UNIT 3

Item #	Answer	Content Focus	CCSS
1	C	Point of View	RL.4.6
2	B	Point of View	RL.4.6
3	A	Vocabulary: Context Clues	L.4.4a
4	C	Point of View	RL.4.6
5	A	Vocabulary: Context Clues	L.4.4a
6	C	Vocabulary: Context Clues	L.4.4a
7	A	Point of View	RL.4.6
8	B	Point of View	RL.4.6
9	A	Author's Point of View	RI.4.8
10	B	Vocabulary: Context Clues	L.4.4a
11	C	Author's Point of View	RI.4.8
12	A	Vocabulary: Context Clues	L.4.4a
13	C	Author's Point of View	RI.4.8
14	C	Author's Point of View	RI.4.8
15	B	Text Features: Time Line	RI.4.7

UNIT 4

Item #	Answer	Content Focus	CCSS
1	C	Point of View	RL.4.6
2	C	Vocabulary: Context Clues	L.4.4a
3	B	Vocabulary: Context Clues	L.4.4a
4	A	Point of View	RL.4.6
5	B	Vocabulary: Context Clues	L.4.4a
6	C	Theme	RL.4.2
7	A	Theme	RL.4.2
8	A	Cause and Effect	RI.4.3
9	C	Cause and Effect	RI.4.3
10	B	Vocabulary: Context Clues	L.4.4a
11	C	Cause and Effect	RI.4.3
12	B	Vocabulary: Context Clues	L.4.4a
13	A	Cause and Effect	RI.4.3
14	B	Cause and Effect	RI.4.3
15	A	Text Features: Diagram	RI.4.7

Exit Assessment · Answer Key

UNIT 5

Item #	Answer	Content Focus	CCSS
1	B	Cause and Effect	RL.4.3
2	A	Cause and Effect	RL.4.3
3	A	Problem and Solution	RL.4.1
4	B	Vocabulary: Context Clues	L.4.4a
5	C	Problem and Solution	RL.4.1
6	A	Cause and Effect	RL.4.3
7	C	Vocabulary: Context Clues	L.4.4a
8	B	Vocabulary: Context Clues	L.4.4a
9	B	Sequence	RI.4.3
10	C	Problem and Solution	RI.4.5
11	C	Sequence	RI.4.3
12	B	Vocabulary: Context Clues	L.4.4a
13	A	Problem and Solution	RI.4.5
14	B	Vocabulary: Context Clues	L.4.4a
15	B	Text Features: Map	RI.4.7

UNIT 6

Item #	Answer	Content Focus	CCSS
1	B	Vocabulary: Context Clues	L.4.4a
2	B	Theme	RL.4.2
3	C	Vocabulary: Context Clues	L.4.4a
4	C	Theme	RL.4.2
5	A	Theme	RL.4.2
6	C	Theme	RL.4.2
7	B	Theme	RL.4.2
8	A	Main Idea and Key Details	RI.4.2
9	C	Vocabulary: Context Clues	L.4.4a
10	A	Main Idea and Key Details	RI.4.2
11	B	Vocabulary: Context Clues	L.4.4a
12	C	Main Idea and Key Details	RI.4.2
13	A	Text Features: Glossary	RI.4.7
14	B	Vocabulary: Context Clues	L.4.4a
15	C	Main Idea and Key Details	RI.4.2

Exit Assessment • Answer Key